'How we respond to adversity in life often defines how the rest of our story unfolds. Jade and John show not just the power of resilience, in *Able to Laugh* but humour as well. It's a wonderfully inspiring story of love, strength and triumph over adversity.'
Simon Thomas, TV presenter, author and president of Blood Cancer UK

'If you like your books full of gritty honesty, laugh-out-loud humour and cheeky but challenging stories about life (including the realities of life with a disability), this is the book for you. But more than that, this is a beautiful story of two people whose love, determination, wit and wisdom are inspiring and hilarious in equal measure. I can't recommend this book highly enough.'
Cathy Madavan, author, speaker and broadcaster

'This book is inspirational. A must-read for any woman who knows the predicament of being a very patient woman with an incredibly annoying husband.'
Suzie Kennedy, actor, singer, comedian and speaker

'We love Jade and John's posts on social media – and now this book! Funny, informative, down-to-earth and hopeful, *Able to Laugh* is a beautiful and moving account of the reality of disability. We recommend it to everyone.'
Archie and Sam Coates, senior leaders at Holy Trinity Brompton

'*Able to Laugh* is a refreshing and honest take on navigating life's challenges with humour and resilience. This book beautifully combines deep reflection, wisdom and wit, offering readers a unique and authentic glimpse into Jade's journey through paralysis as well as their family life. John and Jade's storytelling is engaging and relatable, making this book a must for anyone looking for a heartfelt and entertaining read. *Able to laugh* is a true gem that will leave you laughing, crying and ultimately feeling inspired by the power of laughter in the face of adversity. Highly recommended!'
Dan Blythe, global youth director for Alpha Youth

'This book had me crying tears of sadness, then quickly after tears of joy. It will have you literally laughing out loud in parts. Jade and John are exceptional people who tell their story in a vulnerable, honest and humorous way. This book is one we can all learn and grow from.'
Elle Limebear, singer, songwriter and artist

'Annoyingly, John and Jade are as brilliant at long-form prose as they are at short-form videos. If they decide to do a stand-up tour off the back of this, I am giving up comedy forever.'
Tony Vino, stand-up comedian

'With a mixture of unvarnished honesty and winsome stoicism, Jade and John have produced a super piece of work that never fails to be engaging and always manages to escape the paparazzi of cynicism or triteness that plenty of books in this genre get snapped by. It's a book that's funny when it wants to be, profound when it tries to be, and powerful whether it aims to be or not. It's clearly a book that hasn't been rushed, because this is a story the two of them have been living for some time through the thickness and thinness of life. The care taken to neither shirk nor shy, while remaining unshakeably hopeful, is something that deserves high praise – and so I praise it highly.'
Andy Kind, preacher, author and stand-up comedian

'*Able to Laugh* is a masterpiece of humour, joy and profound wisdom. Jade and John never shy away from the deep and sometimes heartbreaking realities of life – yet it is this authenticity, teamed with genuine humour, that makes their story so uplifting. This book will leave you better for having read it!'
Emma Borquaye, speaker, author and founder of Girl Got Faith

ABLE TO LAUGH

Finding joy though the struggle is real (from TikTok's much-loved interabled couple!)

Jade and John Reynolds

First published in Great Britain in 2024

Society for Promoting Christian Knowledge
The Record Hall, 16–16A Baldwin's Gardens
London, EC1N 7RJ
www.spckpublishing.co.uk

British Library Cataloguing-in-Publication Data
A catalogue record for this book is available from the British Library

ISBN 978–0–281–08981–9
Ebook ISBN 978–0–281–08982–6

3 5 7 9 10 8 6 4 2

Typeset by Fakenham Prepress Solutions
First printed in Great Britain by Clays Limited
Subsequently digitally printed in Great Britain
eBook by Fakenham Prepress Solutions

Produced on paper from sustainable sources

For our cheeky kiddywinks, Elijah and Areli.

You bring us joy, inspire us, boost our social media
career and keep us on our toes/wheels.
P.S. If you guys ever read this, please skip the chapter on sex.

Contents

Introduction: Why did you write a book together?   1

1   Why is your wife in a wheelchair?   7

2   Why can't you walk?   16

3   At least things can't get any worse... can they?   38

4   Do you have a thing for disabled women?   50

5   Is your husband your carer?   67

6   How have you had kids?   77

7   Wasn't it a bit selfish of you to have kids?   92

8   How do you get out of bed in the morning?   103

9   Do any disabled jokes offend you?   113

10   If you're a Christian, why did God let this happen? And why hasn't he healed you?   129

11   If you could go back in time and change what happened to you, would you do it?   137

Acknowledgements   141

Introduction
Q: Why did you write a book together?

A. It was either a book or a third child, so we went with the easy option.

John

Contrary to popular belief, I don't believe laughter is the best medicine. For starters, that's far too broad. It doesn't even mention the condition in need of medicating. There's no 'one size fits all' approach to health. The best medicine for a diabetic, for example, is insulin. If you've been prescribed this book by your doctor, change surgeries immediately. They'll be recommending leeches next. (If you're reading it in the doctor's waiting room, stop being tight, get your phone out and order your own copy. I know waiting times are bad on the NHS, but you're probably not going to make it through the whole book.)

Laughter is a *good* medicine. It won't get to the root of our deepest emotional trauma, but it can play a huge part in helping us cope as we journey towards genuine healing. We know that laughter floods our bodies with feel-good hormones that have big health benefits. We know that laughter opens up our neurological pathways, making us more receptive to other people's ideas and perspectives. We know that laughter is deeply relational and bonds us more closely to those we laugh with. It connects us and it's impossible to hate someone who makes us laugh.

So while this book *is* deep and sad – possibly heartbreaking at times – at its core we think it's funny. And we think that's helpful.

We think you'll be better off for reading it and, most importantly, we think it's *real*. We don't shy away from the times when there isn't much mirth, or fabricate joy when it's absent, but we don't dwell on the crap either. We're just us.

I've been badgering Jade for the best part of a decade to share the story of how she ended up in a wheelchair. It has, in a sense, become part of my story now too. Jade is one of the funniest, most contented people I know. I'm incredibly proud of all she's overcome, and over the past year as we've shared parts of our life online through our comedy/family social media pages, we've been overwhelmed by how many of you have connected with us: @johnejreynolds on all platforms – follow, like, share, subscribe, etc...

Over the course of the last year, we have been asked certain questions over and over again. To begin with, we answered those questions through more videos, but over time, new followers joined our platforms and hadn't seen the historic clips, so still the same questions were asked. We toyed with the idea of making our own website with an FAQ section, but we never got round to it. Besides, a book feels a bit more permanent than a TikTok video. I'm sure it's true that nothing ever really disappears from the internet, but I post around ten videos a week. That's a lot of scrolling for you to find the vintage back catalogue! So, we've pulled out those questions we constantly get on social media and used them as the framework for this book. Each one brings out a chapter of Jade's life/our lives. Think of it as the FAQ section of our website. But longer. In book form. And it costs you money.

This book is, in essence, autobiographical, focusing on Jade's early life, her paralysis journey and our family life. But it's also a book packed full of wisdom (mostly Jade's) and jokes (mostly mine). It is, without a doubt, the best book we've ever written, and if you don't enjoy it, and don't give it a five-star review, I'm pretty sure it means you hate disabled people. No pressure.

So why did we write it? We could answer that in many different ways. But in short, and without me taking *all* the credit, it's mostly because of me. Jade didn't want to write a book.

Jade

I didn't want to write a book…

John

Told you.

Jade

That's not me trying to write an edgy intro or be all 'indie' and aloof. I honestly didn't want to. Those who know me well know I *love* to tell stories (and I've always got about ten new ones!), but despite that, I've never thought of myself as a writer. Also, I was slightly concerned that writing my life story could put my disability centre stage. I know that my story is intriguing, and I realise that there's power in it, but I have to be honest – I cringe a little when I'm described with words like 'inspiring' and I've never wanted to be a poster girl for disability. In fact, I've actively worked hard not to be.

Don't get me wrong, I have a passion for normalising disability, but not for it to become my sole focus or the main thing that defines me. I can't think of anything less normalising than only ever speaking about my wheelchair. I'm still the same person I was before I became paralysed. I just haven't beaten my personal best in the long jump in a while. To speak at length about my disability seemed a bit… one-dimensional.

After much discussion John, and other friends (he's not getting all the credit!), convinced me that the opposite was true. Of course, it's true that our appearance *is* the first thing others notice about us. I can see that when people meet me for the first time they're trying their best not to mention my wheelchair and to act 'normally' while also choosing their language carefully. But for me, the remedy to being reduced to my disability doesn't come through never mentioning it. Ignoring that I'm in a wheelchair can sometimes exacerbate the problem and perpetuate the feeling that it's the elephant in the room. The best way to make sure people don't reduce your whole personhood to just one aspect of your life is by telling your story. I believe the antidote to prejudice is allowing yourself to be known. It may make you feel vulnerable, but I think it's important. It becomes impossible to reduce someone to one feature when you know their whole story – when you know *them*.

John

I wasn't there when Jade became paralysed (your honour). So early parts of the book will probably be a bit 'Jade heavy'. Sorry about that. And yes, positioning your wife's name next to the word 'heavy' in the introduction of an autobiography you've co-written is either stupid or brave. You decide. But I guess it's a good way of seeing if she's proofreading the whole thing or just her parts. If this makes it in, you'll know she hasn't even looked at my input.

I find life stories fascinating, yet it's the lessons that have been learned by those with extraordinary stories that are truly golden to me. Because of that, we want this to be more than just a 'warts and all' account of our life together, Jade's trials and how we manage them. We also want to include some of the things we've learned along the way, and we've sprinkled these throughout the book. We hope that the lessons might help you too, regardless of your background or ability.

In May 2023 it was the twentieth anniversary of the day Jade became paralysed. Anniversaries can be times of precious celebration, but they can also be incredibly painful times of heartbreaking grief. I guess it all depends what you're remembering, doesn't it?

Regardless, though, anniversaries mark important events. And whether those moments have helped us, healed us or hurt us, they have most certainly shaped us. We wouldn't be who we are today without them. That's why remembering them is important – both in being grateful for the good memories, and also in acknowledging the bad and reflecting on what they've taught us and how they've made us stronger. You can't always control what happens to you, but you can control how you respond. Diamonds form under pressure.

Not only did what happened to Jade turn her life upside down, it was really only the beginning. I didn't meet Jade until years later, and what fascinates me most isn't solely what happened to her, but how she navigated it all and what she learned along the way. How did she cope? How was her mental health through it all? As a dad myself now, I wonder how her parents dealt with it. Not just practically, but emotionally. How did she handle the challenge of friendships? The loss of independence? The onset of adolescence as a newly disabled pre-teen? These are questions I've asked Jade over the years, but new questions still surface from time to time, even for me.

Despite having heard her story countless times now, there are still moments when it moves me so very deeply. On the one hand, my heart breaks that she's had to go through everything she's been through, and I wish I could go back in time and make it all OK. On the other hand, I believe these trials have shaped her character, and without them she wouldn't have become the incredible woman she is today – the woman of my dreams.

One of the biggest blessings I've ever received is when she took a chance on me and gave me the opportunity to love her. While I had a lot to learn about her disability, I knew without a doubt I wanted to learn it all. I wanted her story to become *our* story and her world to become *our* world.

I'm so incredibly proud of Jade. I'm proud of her defiant refusal to let her bodily limitations hold her back from living a beautiful life. I'm proud of her for bravely pushing through the moments when no one but me would have known she was scared, and not only did she come out the other side time and time again, but each time she emerged even stronger. I'm proud of her for boldly rebelling against a consumeristic society that regularly puts profits ahead of people and refuses to make the world accessible for all. I'm proud of her for patiently enduring the many frustrations life throws her way without ever becoming resentful or bitter. I'm proud of her for rejecting the labels and limitations others might want to put on her and for never once playing the victim. I'm proud of her for being the most incredible mum to our cheeky monkeys and for her insightfulness in knowing that she wouldn't need working legs to be all the maternal love and support they need. I'm proud of her for sharing her contagious positivity with everyone she meets and for her unwavering faith and the humility to acknowledge that it's God who deserves the credit for how she's thrived. I'm proud of her for getting a book deal and for being willing to share more of her inspiring story with the world. I'm proud of her for exemplifying hope and bringing joy into every room she enters. And most of all, I'm proud of her for being her.

I love you, Jade. I love our life together. I love the family we've made and I'm so proud of you. People say you should never meet your heroes, but I disagree. I got to marry mine.

1

Q: Why is your wife in a wheelchair?

A. Because she can't walk.

John

This is a question I get asked a lot, often directed at me on social media and, sadly, sometimes in person, even with Jade present. Anyone who knows me knows I *love* to talk, but there can surely be no bigger example of mansplaining than an able-bodied man explaining his wife's disability, particularly a disability that preceded their relationship. So I'll (begrudgingly) let her tell her story. After all, she can't walk, but she can talk.

Jade

Right, get comfy, pull up a seat (I've brought my own) and let me share with you what happened that day.

I wonder if you've ever run so fast that you've nearly lost control of your legs? You know – when it feels as if they might even detach from your body and run on without you? If you have, I bet you were a child at the time. I think only children experience that sensation. I've never seen an adult running down a hill, giggling away, and if I did I'd probably be concerned for them. We're either too sensible or too boring. I'm not sure which – perhaps a bit of both. But that's how I ran to the park with my dad and sister that day, totally unaware that it would be the last time I would ever run again. On 13 May 2003, two weeks before my thirteenth birthday, my whole life suddenly and unexpectedly changed for ever.

It was early evening, but still light outside. We'd been at the park for about half an hour when my dad said it was probably best that we head home. I was on the swing at the time, so I jumped off and started to head over to my sister, but weirdly, with each step, it felt as if my legs were getting weaker. It's hard to describe, but it was as though the power was draining out of them. Exhausted, I sat down on the grass, and the moment I hit the ground a pain shot up my thighs that was so excruciating I fell backwards and laid down. After a moment, the agony subsided and my dad did that classic dad thing: 'Jade! The grass is wet. Stop messing around!' With all my strength, I just about managed to get back to my feet. I knew that my legs weren't going to support me for very long, though, so I stumbled over to a bench a few metres away. I sat down and my dad came over and asked what was happening. No matter how I tried, I couldn't get up again. It's now nineteen years on, I'm a mum of two small children, and I have this feeling every single morning. But as a child I was energetic and active. It was bizarre – I knew something was definitely wrong. What I didn't know, when I stumbled over to the bench, was that those would be the last steps I was ever going to take.

Understandably concerned, my dad carried me all the way home, and then took me straight to the hospital, where they ran numerous tests. There was a mixture of confusion and suspicion among the doctors and nurses. One nurse was so convinced I was faking it that she picked me up under my arms and promptly let me go! She assumed my natural reflexes would kick in and I'd save myself. She was wrong. When I crumpled in a heap on the floor, she looked shocked and rushed to get a specialist. Don't worry, my parents did make a complaint.

They decided to admit me into hospital at around midnight and I stayed for the night. I remember the doctors telling me I'd probably be OK to go home in the morning, as there was a good chance it was just a trapped nerve that would sort itself out by the following day, but I felt panicky. Two weeks earlier, I'd watched an episode of the BBC medical drama *Holby City*, where a man became paralysed, and, being the kind of anxious child who didn't even use lifts for fear of getting trapped in one, I was scared. When my sister had been born a few years earlier, my mum was on the twelfth floor of the hospital. I made my dad walk up all twelve flights of stairs when we visited, because I was too terrified to set foot in a lift. I had no idea that, three years later, lifts would become my only option.

With the *Holby City* episode fresh in my worrisome little mind, I remember saying to my dad, 'Oh Dad! I'm not going to be paralysed, am I?' My dad consoled me, 'No, of course not!' I don't think for one second that he was comforting me with a lie. It's possible he didn't want to consider it as an option, but to be honest everyone still thought it was nothing to worry about. We knew that what had happened was weird, but the doctors were all saying I'd probably be off home in the morning.

My dad went home with my little sister, and my mum stayed the night with me. Around three in the morning, my mum checked on me and as she leaned on my bed, it was damp. Not only was I unable to walk, but to make matters worse someone had weed all over my bed! To make matters worse still, apparently it was me. Since I'd been admitted hours earlier, I hadn't been able to feel or move my legs, and as a result I had no idea I'd wet the bed. My mum called the nurses, and they rushed me down for an emergency MRI scan. It became clear that everyone considered this an emergency as the MRI technician remarked that she was getting a flight at 8 a.m. to go on holiday, but they'd called her in to do the urgent scan. In the early hours, we were all too disoriented to properly register what was going on. I mostly remember being terrified of the MRI scanner, which is essentially a noisy horizontal lift, albeit a stationary one. Back then, they didn't provide headphones with music like they do today. To distract myself from the loud noise and the terrifying situation, I remember humming Christian worship songs in an attempt to feel some peace.

Frustratingly, every test and scan I had over the first few weeks showed no indication of any problems. Eventually my blood tests started to show that something was wrong, although no one was sure of the nature of the problem. They also had no idea if the paralysis would travel up my body, but they seemed confident that it wouldn't be permanent. At worst, they thought I might walk with a limp. It seems almost comical now, but at thirteen I was absolutely mortified at the idea of needing a walking stick like an old lady! I remember the nurses trying to sell the idea to me, saying, 'Oh well, you might just drag one leg behind the other a little bit, but you'll be OK.' I vowed I would never set foot in school again. This, to be fair, was a promise I kept.

Being bed bound on a children's ward, I ended up watching all the comings and goings of other children and comparing my situation with that of those around me. Sometimes they'd be in and out in a few days with something straightforward (and frankly pathetic), like a broken bone. Amateurs. Other times they were regular visitors. I remember an eight-year-old called Ellie, who was in regularly with brittle bone disease. She seemed so comfortable, almost at home, in the hospital environment and I was thankful that I was on my first ever inpatient experience.

I ended up staying in hospital for six weeks before they were able to diagnose what was wrong with me. They concluded it was something called acute transverse myelitis. It's classified as an auto-immune condition and it's so rare that they still don't know what causes it. So rare, in fact, that the doctors said I had more chance of winning the lottery than suffering from it. Given that, being a child, I wasn't even legally able to buy a lottery ticket, I think we can all agree that that is incredibly rare. It's just a theory, but it was thought that I had a common virus, and as my immune system went to attack the problem it accidentally started to attack my own spinal cord. This made it swell and it began to rub against the vertebrae in my back. This in turn damaged the covering (myelin sheath) of my spinal cord. The signals going from my brain could no longer continue down to my legs. If you're struggling to visualise it, think about when the plastic covering on the wire of your phone charger starts to fray and you know it's only a matter of time before the charger itself stops working. Basically, I'd short-circuited. Some people recover from it; others don't. I was one of the unfortunate ones.

I remember vividly, about a month after my diagnosis, Cathy White my consultant, the registrar, and a team of doctors gathered in my room. Cathy asked me, 'Do you know what we are here to tell you, Jade?'

I calmly replied, 'Yes, that I'm never going to walk again.'

The room fell silent. 'Well, yes,' Cathy hesitantly confirmed.

I think they expected me to break down in tears or scream in denial, but to be honest with you I had already accepted that it was the most probable outcome. In fact, it's how I continue to process things to this day – coming to terms with the worst-case scenario and finding peace with that helps me cope. I think it's something many wheelchair users have in common. The seemingly unending disappointments that come our way teach us not to get our hopes up. Whether it's bad medical news, no appropriate wheelchair access to a venue, or (my favourite) shops with their disabled toilets full of boxes of stock, disabled people live in a world where disappointments aren't in short supply. But we'll talk more about that later.

In the coming weeks and months, I was regularly offered psychological assessments and anti-depressants, which initially frustrated me and over time actually made me quite cross. I wasn't depressed. Obviously, I wasn't jumping for joy (or jumping for anything), but I was coming to terms with things in my own way. I was upset at times, but I also had some moments of real happiness and fun with the friends I made and the nurses who supported me. Looking back, I'm quite impressed at my own self-awareness and willingness to just sit with my emotions. I recognised that numbing the pain through medication wasn't the correct solution for me and for how I was feeling. Of course, I'm not saying that anti-depressants or mental health medication isn't a good idea for those who need it. I just didn't.

In total, I ended up living in hospital for four months before I could return home and the work of adapting our house began, but I'll save that for the next chapter.

John

I have to be honest – and don't judge me – I'm so used to hearing this story that I can feel as though it's lost its impact on me. I've heard Jade recount the tale for curious people countless times over the years. I'm so familiar with it now that sometimes I just sort of zone out. Other times, though, it still has the power to hit me right in the heart. I've just had one of those moments reading Jade's reply to the consultant, 'I'm never going to walk again.' It made me hugely emotional. This was particularly embarrassing, as we're currently writing together in the coffee shop area of a kids' soft play centre. (With our kids, obviously. Not because we write better with a backdrop of a hundred screaming children.)

While I've heard it a lot, Jade's story still feels surreal to me. I've only ever known Jade to be a wheelchair user. The woman I fell in love with was already disabled and so, at times, it's weird for me to imagine her ever walking at all. I remember visiting her home in Swansea when we'd been dating for about six months, and her family put on old home videos. About five minutes in, after seeing Jade walk, I was overcome with emotion and I just burst into tears. It was a very 'alpha' moment for me and I think it really demonstrated to her dad that Jade had chosen a strong, stable, masculine man.

You've probably started to realise (as anyone who knows her well certainly does) that Jade is strong, confident, sassy and very self-assured, and even as her husband that's what I see 90% of the time. It's not an image she projects or a defence mechanism; it's just who she is. So much so that I can sometimes forget that it was ever tough for her. I can forget that she was a thirteen-year-old child when she went through this trauma. The strong woman I fell in love with was once a vulnerable child going through considerable physical and emotional pain. That breaks my heart but also blows my mind in equal measure, to see the woman she has become despite, and possibly because of, all she has had to endure.

Jade

Pain is part of the plan

Throughout this book I share some reflections I've had over the years. Not because I believe disability turned me into 'the all-knowingly enlightened one', but because I believe my experiences may be helpful to others. Often, when we go through trauma, we're in survival mode. We're just doing our best to get by. It's only over time that we're able to observe the situation from a safe distance. We can look back more objectively, and see the period for what it actually was. So my reflections in this book aren't necessarily how I was feeling in the middle of becoming paralysed, but rather those of a thirty-four-year-old woman who has been disabled for more than twenty years. My hope is that they carry the wisdom of experience, and the encouragement that life, although different, can be good again for all who go through a life-changing event.

One question I'm often asked is: 'How have you coped so well, despite all that you've been through?'

I think the answer to that can be found in the combination of my outlook on life and the hope I find through my Christian faith. In fact, I believe my outlook on life is shaped so fundamentally *by* my faith that it is impossible to separate the two. Fear not, however, these reflections won't be 'preachy'. You won't need to be a Christian or disabled to find them helpful, and I'm not going to beat you over the head with a Bible (or a medical journal). Rather they are advice, based on my experience, that I believe is helpful for anyone and everyone. Even John found them helpful, and I honestly thought he was beyond help.

One lesson I have learned is that life is unpredictable. I dare say it's a lesson you have learned in your own life too. We never know what's going to come our way. Through no fault of my own and without warning, I went from living a 'normal', happy, healthy life to being a paraplegic wheelchair user. Life can be cruel and its unpredictability can be terrifying. Any control freaks out there?

Hey! How are you feeling right now? Do you need a paper bag to breath into?

How can we respond? Because respond we must. Pastor Charles Swindoll once said, 'Life is 10% what happens to you and 90% how you react.'[1] While I'm not entirely sure of his statistics, his point works for me. If we want to survive, or better yet thrive, we must be more concerned with what we *can* control than what we can't. Who has ever solved a problem by worrying about it? Seriously, have you? If you have a big exam coming up, which strategy works best: creating a revision timetable or scheduling in a good old worry session? When you need to have a tough chat with your boss, what's the most effective way to prepare: chatting it through with a wise friend and coming up with an action plan, or staying up until 2 a.m. overthinking it, wracked with anxiety?

As Jesus put it, 'Can any one of you, by worrying, add a single hour to your life?' (Matthew 6:27). Or as A. J. Cronin, the Scottish novelist, writes: 'Worry never robs tomorrow of its sorrow, but only saps today of its strength.'[2]

I'm fully aware that this is easier said than done. Like many lessons, we already know it's true, but putting it into practice requires... well, practice. Because fear is something that can plague many of us – whether it's fear of spiders, walking home alone, the unknown, clowns, the dentist, unknown clown dentists, the list goes on. Whether they are phobias or totally rational, it's hard to live a fear-free life.

And fear isn't in and of itself bad. Rational fears protect us. I think there's some pretty dodgy advice out there on fear. Something I used to hate was the claim that FEAR stands for False Evidence Appearing Real. That might be accurate for *irrational* fear, but not for all fear. Aristotle is often quoted as saying, 'Fear is pain arising from the anticipation of evil', which paints a more honest and nuanced picture. It's true that it might be irrational, but it might be

---

1   Charles R. Swindoll, *Life Is 10% What Happens to You and 90% How You React* (Nashville, TN: Thomas Nelson, 2023).

2   A. J. Cronin, quoted in *Today's Gift: Daily Meditations for Families* (Hazelden Publishing, 1985), p. 11.

perfectly legitimate. Labelling all fear as false leads us to avoid our legitimate feelings. We can't deal with anything we don't acknowledge. In fact, fear can help us make wise choices and motivate us to be correctly cautious when danger arises. So perhaps it might be helpful to ask yourself here, 'Do I *experience* fear or do I live in a place of fear?' Is fear an occasional visitor or is it a permanent house mate? And when you do experience it, are you overcome by it? Because many of us find ourselves living limited lives, not out of sensible caution, but because we're controlled by fear.

This is where my faith really helps me, particularly when I read in the Bible that God says, `Do not fear, because I am with you' (Isaiah 41:10). Now, I want to quickly say, when God says, 'Do not fear,' this isn't a moral command that we must not break. For one thing, psychologists tell us that feelings like fear and attraction are reflexes that can't be avoided. They're primary instincts, and nowhere does the Bible condemn the natural response of our primary instincts. Additionally, if it is wrong to feel fear, then Jesus messed up big time when he was so afraid of the crucifixion that he sweated drops of blood. If Jesus is allowed to be afraid, I'm pretty sure we are. Rather than the Bible painting a picture of God as an angry disciplinarian scolding the fearful, we actually see a loving Father comforting his children, as he continues by saying that the reason we don't need to fear is because he is with us. The discouragements away from fear aren't encouragements for us to pretend life isn't tough or terrifying at times. The encouragement for me is that, with God in my life, I know fear doesn't have the final say, and I'm not going to let it hold me back or rob me of my future. Jesus feels the fear of the cross, but still goes through with God's plan for him.

I believe that God has a plan for my life, and is with each of us through all our struggles and fears. We cannot change our past, so let's not worry away our present and limit our future.

2

Q: Why can't you walk?

A. Because I'm disabled.

Jade

I've already mentioned my calm reaction to being told I was never going to walk again. Aside from my faith, I think it's also possible that I maintained my composure because it was all a bit surreal. Anyone who's had life-changing news will tell you that there's no way of knowing all the implications or situational struggles you will go on to endure when you're first told. The accompanying frustrations and difficulties are more incremental than that – and thank goodness they are, because if in that moment I had been made aware of every single struggle I was going to experience, it would have been completely overwhelming.

My time in hospital was obviously very challenging, but those first few months were just the beginning of the journey. For anyone, rehabilitation and recovery (however possible that is) require hard work and take time.

Every paraplegic's injury is as unique as their fingerprint. How their body reacts depends on the severity and location of the injury. This is known as the level. The higher up the damage to the spinal cord, the more of the body it affects. I know you're not here for an anatomy class, so I'll keep this brief. Basically your spine has four different categories. Working down from the top, there's the cervical spine (the neck area), the thoracic spine (your upper back), the lumbar spine (your lower back) and the sacral area (your sacrum and coccyx). Everyone with a spinal cord injury will be assessed by MRI scan, to work out where their injury lies on their spine. Those with injuries to their cervical spine at the top will have some level of tetraplegia. This can range from full paralysis in all limbs and trunk, along with difficulty breathing and speaking, to paralysis in the limbs but with some movement and the ability to still grasp and release. Those with thoracic, lumbar or sacral injuries will have their lower body affected. This can range from full paraplegia to being able to walk, but with some loss of function in hips and legs. The spinal injury is given a letter that corresponds to the area it's in (C, T, L or S) and a number that corresponds to the vertebrae within that area (C1-8, T1-12, L1-5, S1-5).

How are you holding up? Still with me? After that crash course, you'll probably be interested to know that my injury was between T7 and T10. The damage caused runs across four vertebrae. In addition, it wasn't 'complete'; that is to say my spinal cord wasn't severed at one particular location, because my injury wasn't caused through an accident or trauma but through inflammation.

Most people think that when you suffer a spinal cord injury, the only real issue is that you can't walk or you lose aspects of mobility. In reality, there is a whole host of accompanying bodily functions that are affected and need careful management. These could include reduced bladder and bowel function, reduced sexual function, difficulty with temperature regulation, poor circulation, pain, spasms and more.

For me, most of those areas have been affected to some degree. To urinate, I have to self-catheterise with a 'speedy cath compact' – which sounds like a make-up kit you'd get for a quid by the counter in a pharmacy. I was told that the packaging looks like a little lip gloss, so if it falls out of your bag you won't be embarrassed. It's actually a small tube you insert inside your urethra to keep it open so that you can fully empty your bladder and reduce the likelihood of infections and bladder stones. It's quick and I'm very used to it now, but to begin with it was pretty overwhelming. The sensation of needing the toilet was dulled, and my bladder control became weaker. This did lead to a few accidents in the early days, which as you can imagine was very embarrassing.

None of this was helped by my vulnerability to urine infections, meaning the doctors told me to drink lots throughout the day. One of the medical professionals made the mistake of telling my mum this, who became a hydration micromanager. She insisted I down a glass of water every thirty minutes. It got so crazy, I started inventing ways of redistributing my fluids. Like a child spooning her vegetables onto a sibling's plate when they weren't looking, I started pouring my water into nearby plants, the commode, and even smuggling it into the shower with me. I was like the prisoners in *The Great Escape*, when they attached the special pouches to their trousers, allowing them to scatter sand out the bottom as they walked around the camp.

In case you think I'm exaggerating, one time, while the nurses in the hospital were measuring my urine output to check all was functioning correctly, my mum held up the measuring jug of my pee and proudly declared, 'That's the best yet!' as if I'd just broken a world record at the Olympics… or the Paralympics. It was more than one litre in a single pee! Far from being happy, the nurses were horrified, and told my mum that those were kidney-damaging levels of wee. She calmed down a bit after that.

So that's wee chat. Are you ready for poo talk? Good. Buckle in. These days, you'll be pleased to know, I have regular bowel movements, but when I was originally paralysed that wasn't the case. This was most likely due to the shock of the injury. My digestive system seemed to stop functioning for the first week. And then the second week. And then the third. I knew things weren't right on my birthday, when I struggled to eat even a slice of cake. Usually, my cake-related struggles involve restraining myself from eating the whole thing. Something had to be very wrong.

Things got so bad that I had people praying for my poo. I'm not joking. I don't think it was a notice in the church newsletter, but it wasn't far off.

John

And when Jade says 'praying for my poo' she doesn't mean they were laying hands on the poo itself. She means they were praying for her to be able to poo. That was probably obvious to many, but if social media has taught me anything, it is never to assume people understand.

Jade

So, I was sitting on the toilet for one hour twice a day – they were that desperate for something to happen. Now, if this was my husband, that would be quite a quick one for him. Why do men take *so* long to have a poo? I don't know if they're avoiding the kids or getting distracted on their phones, or is that just how long men take?! But I'm talking 2003, so way before iPhones. There was no playing *Candy Crush* or scrolling through social media. I just sat there. My stomach was rock solid for weeks and I started to feel really unwell. Until…

One day, after finishing my shower, around the four-week mark, my mum wheeled me back towards my bedroom in the shower wheelchair. One thing you need to know about the shower wheelchair is that it has a hole in the seat to stop water pooling. You may be able to see where this is going – and where I was about to. As she was wheeling, she suddenly remarked, 'What's that noise?' It sounded like someone had dropped a chocolate gateau. We looked down and realised that the much-anticipated moment had arrived. Not in my bedroom, but on Bay 2, the open ward. You know – *probably the busiest unit in the hospital. During visiting time.*

Children were pointing. Mums gagged. Old ladies keeled over. Or that's what you'd expect. But actually this was in Britain. Nobody really reacted at all. The nurses rushed to help, but everyone else just pretended nothing was going on. It was just the elephant in the room. Complete with elephant-sized droppings. It was like a gross version of Hansel & Gretel. Nothing to see here, just a fun game of follow the faeces – back to my bedroom.

In the rush to my room, my mum stepped in it and realised she'd wheeled the chair through it too. As she tried to manoeuvre me onto the bed, there was now a constant stream of excrement. It must have looked like a sausage-maker had got jammed on full power. By this point my mum had not only stepped in it, but knelt and leaned in it too. She looked like the victim of a paintball drive-by. The nurses rushed to get a disposable sheet to put underneath me so my mum could tag them in and clean herself up. It was carnage. We're talking *that* scene from *Bridesmaids*. If it wasn't such a relief, I'd have probably been mortified. I felt so light afterwards and instantly better. It was a weight off my mind and my stomach. Plus it prepared me perfectly for two pregnancies later down the line. By which I mean a heavy, solid stomach, and not because I regularly pooed myself while pregnant.

I think that's another reason many people who have been through severe health struggles have such a good sense of humour; when you go through hard times, you're constantly humbled and forced to take life less seriously. It also helps enormously when you have wonderful and outgoing medical professionals around you. The team at Morriston Hospital in Swansea were fantastic.

Regarding the other complications I mentioned above – sexual function, temperature regulation, poor circulation, pain, spasms and the like – we'll look at some of those in the coming chapters.

One big hurdle every person with a significant spinal injury must overcome is learning to control their body again when it suddenly feels totally different. I remember a few people asking me, 'Do you ever forget you can't walk any more and try to stand up? Or go to get up out of your chair?' But you don't. When half of your body is paralysed, it's essentially a dead weight. You feel constantly weighted down in the chair, and you can't forget it. Added to that, I have an almost constant sensation of pins and needles in my legs and feet, much like when your mouth is thawing out after a visit to the dentist. It doesn't feel normal and it doesn't exactly feel painful, but I can still feel something. This can draw my attention to it more, so for me at least it's impossible to forget it.

When the hospital ran tests to see my level of feeling, they had a tool with a sharp end and a blunt end, which they used to prod my legs. I had to close my eyes and try to tell them which end I thought they were using. Nine times out of ten, if I concentrated, I could tell the difference between the two. But they realised I couldn't tell the difference between hot and cold – even very extreme temperatures – and my legs weren't sensitive enough to feel the pain of a jab or the pleasure of a tickle. I was told I should probably get leg and foot massages to help with my circulation, but I just find it too overstimulating. The sensation is so odd that my brain can't cope with the irritation.

Once it was established that I wasn't going to make a full recovery, the focus switched to rehabilitation and helping me work towards independence. I had to start with the basics like relearning to balance. My centre of gravity had changed. Many people don't think about how crucial your leg muscles are to your stability, not just when you're standing but also when you're sitting down. For those who are able-bodied, shifting their weight is intuitive and they use their thighs, stomach muscles and glutes to compensate for any changes in position. But when I became paralysed, I no longer had access to those muscles. Unlike with walking, there were times when I forgot that reaching with my upper body still required the strength of my lower body – a strength I no longer had. It was common for me to try to reach for my drink, or something on a nearby table, and topple onto my side on the bed. When this happened early on, I would just be stuck there, lying awkwardly and, if I could reach my button, I'd call for the nurse.

And so began my physiotherapy. Honestly, I hated it. Not my physiotherapist, she was lovely, but the work was gruelling. To regain my balance, I had to practise catching a ball without falling over. My hand–eye co-ordination wasn't the best when I *could* walk, so I wasn't a fan of switching to expert mode when I already struggled on beginner. As if that wasn't bad enough, I remember being surprised one week to arrive at physiotherapy to find two very good-looking student physios who were there on placement to practise with the patients. Why is it always when you're at your worst that the hot guys show up? And why, in the middle of one of the toughest moments of my life, did I still care about impressing boys? As I'm sure you can imagine, it's quite hard to impress a crush when you're a newly disabled, goofy, thirteen-year-old paraplegic girl in an Eeyore nightie and surgical stockings. You would not have described me as a catch. Physio pun intended.

Another element of my physio sessions involved them strapping me into a standing frame, a contraption that wouldn't have seemed out of place alongside the rest of the torture devices in the Tower of London. It was made entirely of wood, apart from the leather belts to lock me into place. Its purpose was to encourage weight-bearing and help with bone density and circulation. It was probably the weirdest and most boring hour of every day. If I had become paralysed today, I know I'd have been more co-operative with the physios and more motivated to follow their advice and do the best for my body. But that isn't always the attitude you have as a teenager. In general, I was quite resistant to those physiotherapy sessions. It felt very emotional to me, perhaps because I was forced to confront my disability head on and I couldn't pretend everything was OK. The only time I was keen to attend was when I had purposely arranged for my tutor to come at the same time. I'd be in physio thinking that at least I'd avoided maths that week. After that happened a few times, the nurses on the ward cottoned on to my devious little plan and told me to stop double-booking myself. I tried to claim that I was so bad at maths I didn't even know what 'double' meant, but they were having none of it.

I also had hydrotherapy (which I hated), wheelchair skills (which was quite fun) and general exercise (which I hated). One of the hardest things I found, though, wasn't even a physical struggle, but a relational one. Going through something so rare and unique is an incredibly isolating experience. Not just physically, because I couldn't see my friends at school, but also because there were very few people who could really relate to what I was going through.

Even in the hospital, many of the other children only needed to be there short term, so I was very used to the faces changing in the beds next to me – because they were discharged from hospital, I mean, not because they'd had some sort of facial surgery. Of course I was happy that they got to leave, and I didn't resent them for it, but it was a constant reminder of my own lack of improvement, which meant I couldn't go home.

Even my parents got to leave the hospital and have a break from it all, but the struggle was inescapable for me. Don't get me wrong, my parents were absolutely incredible, and I realise that even more so now, as I reflect back on that time as a parent myself. Not only did I have a four-year-old sister they needed to look after, but obviously they also had all the other adult responsibilities of work and life and a home to maintain and now adapt. Sometimes I don't know how my parents did it. I think they came in every day for two months before they finally took a day to decompress. I remember feeling so upset that day at the time, but now I get it. I feel I need a break from *my* kids every eight minutes some days, let alone every eight weeks, and that's without all the stress of one of them being ill. However, at the time I remember thinking, 'It's all right for you. I wish *I* could have a break from this!'

However, when my family couldn't, my church could. It's sort of one of the perks of being part of a church community – there's a large group of lovely, selfless people who want to visit, support, send cards and gifts and just generally show love in a wide variety of ways. I remember the nurses regularly commenting on how popular I was because my church, Cornerstone in Swansea, which we'd been a part of since I was six, really went the extra mile. It was essentially as if I had dozens of aunties, uncles and grandparents – an extended family – who were there for me and my family when we needed them most.

Not only were they there for me in general ways, but there was also a wide variety of expertise within our church. If I needed blocky blonde highlights that were all the rage, Pam was a hairdresser. My legs waxed? Sian was a beautician. My stock of Welsh cakes replenished? There were seventeen old ladies who loved to smuggle in contraband. Getting my legs waxed as a paraplegic was actually the first time I realised there were advantages to not being able to feel!

On top of the practical support, we were also prayed for regularly. Often the nurses would walk in while some of my church family were praying for me. I think they found it unusual at first, but as time went on I could tell they found it really touching. To begin with, the prayers focused on my healing (and we'll discuss my thoughts on that in another chapter). While I've continued to receive prayer for healing over the years, life doesn't stop if you aren't healed, so prayers for peace and medical support were also a huge help.

The support I got was incredible and I honestly don't think my family and I would have coped without our church. Yet one of the biggest struggles was still the isolation. Not in terms of visitors – I had lots – but in terms of people I could relate to, who *truly* knew what I was going through.

One person who understood me was Andrea Evans. Confident, outgoing and open, Andrea was a patient and a huge support to me. She'd been in hospital for several months by the time I was admitted in May, so she was further on from me in her journey. She was also four years older than me, so I couldn't help but look up to her. I think she was admitted the October before me after contracting meningitis and septicaemia. As a result, she was in ICU for a while and initially they thought she wouldn't make it. Thankfully she pulled through, but was left with severely damaged legs as a result of the septicaemia. Despite all the trauma she'd been through, I remember her sense of humour and how she used it to cope. It reminded me of my own family.

The day after my birthday, Andrea opted for a double amputation. She knew that her legs were so damaged she would never be able to walk unaided again. They were causing her such pain that the doctors suggested amputation as an option. She decided to take it. I remember thinking what a brave decision that was. I admired her courage and fortitude.

Most of us would probably rest up after such a major surgery, but what felt like a matter of weeks later, Andrea went camping! Looking back, I'm so grateful she was placed in my life, because she taught me, right from the word go, that life doesn't end just because you have a chronic illness.

It's essential to have people to look up to in life. I think, for all of us, there are pioneers who show us what we can achieve and give us that vision of goodness we can set our sights on. It's for this reason that I love the story of Roger Bannister. Roger was the first man to break the four-minute mile in 1954. Before his achievement it was widely believed to be impossible. It requires maintaining an average speed of 15 m.p.h. for a whole mile – that's epically fast. However, once Roger broke the record for the first time in human history, it took only two months for another person to do the same. As of June 2022, 1,755 athletes had broken the four-minute barrier. I'm well aware of the irony of comparing Andrea, a girl with no legs, to Roger Bannister, but she helped me to form the positive attitude that I have today and helped me to believe I could have a 'normal' life, just like Roger inspired another 1,754 people to run ridiculously fast. Once someone showed me I could push back on the boundaries the world put in place for me, I felt that nothing was out of my reach. It chimed with my spirit.

I'll always remember sharing a room with Andrea for a few nights. Not long after her amputations, we were told there was a room with two beds in it if we wanted it, so we… well, we didn't 'jump' at the chance, but we were really keen to be roommates. I remember one night she was complaining that her feet were cold. 'Andrea, you haven't got any feet!' I laughed.

'I know,' she said, 'but they *feel* cold!' She was experiencing a fascinating but pretty common phenomenon among amputees called 'phantom limb pain'. We couldn't stop giggling as we called a nurse to put a blanket where her feet would have been.

Returning to home and school

Returning to school in the September was nerve-racking. We'd had loads of meetings about accessibility, health and safety and the school's provision of a learning support officer (LSO). It was clear things were going to be very different for me. My school friends had visited me a couple of times during the four months I was in hospital. While we all had mobile phones, these were the days when texts cost 10 pence and there were no smart phones with social media yet, so there was no constant messaging back and forth or group chats. Once you were bored of playing *Snake* you just put your phone down. Crazy, right?

When I returned, there were a whole load of factors that made my friendships suddenly very different. The biggest struggle wasn't solely my disability, but how the world changed to accommodate me. I now had my LSO with me 24/7. Well, from 9 a.m. to 3:30 p.m. (they didn't come home with me). Unsurprisingly, teenage girls don't feel especially comfortable divulging all the latest school gossip in front of an adult, so while we still hung out it wasn't as natural as before. The school yard was typically chaotic with boys playing football and, to my thirteen-year-old mind, being immature idiots, so I mostly stayed indoors, isolating myself even more.

To begin with I was a big novelty. Everyone wanted the inside scoop on how I'd become paralysed. They knew a swing was involved, and people started saying I'd attempted a loop the loop and fudged it, landing on my head and severing my spinal cord. As the rumours already ranged from the sublime to the ridiculous, I started to fuel the gossip, just for the bants. Bitten by a shark, attacked by ninjas, the victim of a drive-by perpetrated by the head of maths because I was failing his class and bringing down the grade average – these were just some of the tales that echoed through the corridors. And that was just the staffroom gossip from the teachers! Even the dinner ladies wanted me to spill the tea. I remember one looking at me perplexed and asking, 'What you done, gal?' At first I thought I was being accused of a school crime, but then I realised she meant why was I in a wheelchair? On that occasion I did tell the truth, but for the most part I had some fun with it. When you're constantly met with people feeling entitled to answers, you get bored and frustrated, so I was like the Joker in *Batman*, giving everyone a different story of how I got my scars.

The teachers were incredibly nice to me. I lost count of how many times a teacher announced in a big loud voice in front of my class, 'And it's *so* great to have Jade Greasley back with us. Jade, we really missed you when you were gone. We were all thinking of you and it's so great you've managed to get back to school and brighten our days with your lovely face once again.'

I know. Absolutely mortifying.

Whenever there was a whole-class detention, I was exempt. This would have been fine, but so that I wasn't alone, the teacher always let me choose a friend. Lovely gesture, right? Wrong. Every time I was given that power, twenty-nine heads would spin around, and twenty-nine sets of pleading eyes would be willing me to pick them. These fell into a few categories. There were the stoner boys who never made any effort with me, and knew in their hearts they weren't getting selected, yet still had a glazed look of optimism – if only because it would have meant getting out early to roll another joint. Then there were the unrealistic optimists – those who had smiled and held a door open for me six months ago and were clinging to the one interaction we'd ever had, hoping that would swing it for them. Then there were my four best friends, each of whom could have rightfully asked me, 'Why didn't you pick me?' if I went for another person. In the end, I had to draw up a rota for them, just to keep the peace.

I know that the teachers were just being encouraging and welcoming, and actually as an adult I think it was very sweet. But I wasn't an adult then. I was thirteen, and every time they did allow me to skip the punishment, I wanted the ground to just open up and swallow… them. I was desperate for normality and to blend in again. It only further highlighted how different I now was.

Even when they tried to do something to help me feel better about the situation, like excluding me from detentions, it inadvertently made me feel worse. Before the injury, pupils had been separated into two groups: boys and girls. The toilets, changing rooms and PE classes all saw us divided up. Suddenly I entered the 'other' category, not really fitting in anywhere.

I returned at the beginning of Year 9, and between Years 9 and 12, my attendance record was incredibly low. I think around the 20% mark. If you strongly dislike school, I thoroughly recommend paralysis. No one questioned a thing!

Seriously, though, I'm going to share future struggles more in an upcoming chapter, but the paralysis was only the beginning of my health issues – as is the case for many people who become paralysed. As my paralysis was not 'complete', one side of my body had better-developed muscles than the other. This led to scoliosis – a curvature of my spine. It caused me a lot of pain. I was constantly bent over like a prawn in need of a good back crack. To rectify this, I had a plaster cast made of my torso, so physios could provide me with a bespoke, thick leather corset! A far cry from the delicate, flattering corsets of today – this was more like a saddle. Put me in a turbo-charged electric wheelchair and I could have won the Grand National. Veganism wasn't as big back then, but today I can imagine being hated for sporting half a cow around my midriff. I had to wear it in all weather conditions as well. It was uncomfortable in winter and sweltering in summer. It was yet another visible sign of my imperfect body and it made me incredibly self-conscious. I'd wear loose-fitting jumpers to cover it all year round.

When I was asked what colour I wanted for the leather harness (and was given a palette of options that would have bored a colour-blind librarian) I asked for pink. It wasn't a Barbie pink, more of a blush pink, but to be honest it wasn't really about the hue. It was about having some element of control over my chaotic life. To have the pink trimmings was like rolling a turd in glitter, but psychologically it was a battle won for me. I can't tell you how much I needed that at the time.

I remember returning for adjustments to be made and the team telling me that since they'd made my pink one they'd had other girls see mine and ask for pink! I remember feeling quite the trendsetter and something of a pioneer. Was I comparable to Roger Bannister? That's not for me to comment, but let's just say that Roger never pulled off pink like I did. I've seen the photos – he mostly just wore black and white. So dull.

I don't have lots of fun memories of school. The social isolation, coupled with the pain of scoliosis, made enjoying classes difficult. However, that improved in sixth form.

Sixth form

In the February of 2007, towards the end of Year 12, I had surgery to correct my scoliosis. I'll go into greater detail later, but in short my spine was so curved that my ribs and hips were touching.

Without the surgery, it would have eventually crushed my lungs. (My health struggles have threatened to take my breath away more than John ever has.) I'd known from the age of fourteen that this surgery would be necessary. The medical professionals had made three things clear: first, it was essential surgery if I didn't want to die a slow and painful death. I decided I didn't. Second, it was major surgery that wasn't without its risks. I would need two operations within a week, which would mean being under anaesthetic for up to twenty hours in total. Third, I couldn't have the surgery until I'd finished growing. This meant that it had been an ominous cloud hanging over me for three years. While I waited, I just had to manage my symptoms as best I could – with my pink saddle corset.

I had to repeat Year 12 because the post-surgery recovery time meant I missed all my AS-level exams. It was annoying, but deep down I was chuffed, as it meant that I could be in all the same classes as Tifanie, one of my closest friends at the time.

Once the surgery was over and done with I managed to really enjoy school. As soon as I had recovered, I immediately investigated driving lessons. I know what you're thinking – how do I do the pedals? They had to implant a small microchip into my brain and then a sensor into the pedals so that whenever I think 'accelerate' or 'break' the car knows what to do. Just kidding. But this is what I told inquisitive students at school, and I think many of them believed it. In reality, it's just a hand-controls system. The car has to be automatic and then a specialist car mechanic can adapt the car so that whenever I pull my hand-control lever to the right of the steering wheel, the car accelerates and whenever I push it, it breaks.

I'm never annoyed that people are surprised I can drive. I didn't even know I would be able to until I met another wheelchair user at a Christian conference when I was fifteen. I remember chatting to her about how she'd made her way there and she said she'd driven down. I was shocked! But from that day I knew, as soon as I was able to, I was going to learn. John didn't pass his test until he was twenty-eight *and* he failed the first time. Just thought you should know.

The freedom that driving brought me was life-changing. After years of feeling stuck – in hospital, in my bedroom, in the lounge, in a classroom, at break time, in my wheelchair – suddenly the world opened up to me. When you're disabled, you're allowed to learn to drive a year early. I was one of the first to pass my driving test in my year and suddenly… hello, Miss Popular! Finally, having wheels was a plus. At least at first. Over time, the number of 'begs' became frustrating. I remember a mouthy Year 10 boy giving me his McDonald's order. I said, 'Who are you? This isn't Meals on Wheels, mate! Off you go!'

I finished school with two As and a C in my A-levels, including 100% in my RE exam. I don't mean to highlight that to manipulate you, but I'm pretty sure it means you have to agree with all of the faith advice I give you in this book. My teacher was ecstatic and burst into the common room singing 'The Only Way Is Up' by Yazz in celebration. On reflection, it was a celebration that didn't actually make much sense, as technically the only way is down from 100%, but there isn't a song for that. She was delighted and I was incredibly proud of myself.

It was one of the first moments to give me hope that despite the extra hardships and hurdles I had to overcome, I didn't have to let them hold me back. I could still achieve a lot in life.

John

It was probably what gave her the hope of landing me. If you can get 100% in an A-level, you can probably bag a 10/10 husband too. (What? Did you really think you wouldn't hear from me again in this chapter?)

Jade

Don't worry about John; you'll learn to tune him out like I have. Now, back to the story. Not only did I have to adjust to school but, as any teenage girl will know, life-changing trauma or no life-changing trauma, those years are tough. You're contending with things like hormones, body changes, self-image and peer pressure.

Our body image can be negatively affected and distorted because of our culture's obsession with perfection. And that's only got worse since the rise of social media. I knew I could never live up to our culture's beauty standards. At first, that was very frustrating. I was naturally slim and therefore fortunate that clothes often suited me, and I loved fashion. But most clothes are made to look good standing up. It's called the 'catwalk', after all, not the 'cat sit'. There was a frustrating and at times demoralising readjustment that I needed to make. Some fashions were no longer an option for me, and some were borderline scandalous. You cannot wear a mini-skirt in a wheelchair without it looking as though you've gone out in just a belt.

My body changed dramatically after becoming paralysed. The muscles in my legs atrophied and became skinny, and my upper body grew more muscular from pushing my chair. I remember feeling very aware of the differences in the beginning, comparing my body to the those of the people around me. We were teenagers, so everyone was hyper-aware of how we were changing, except that my body was changing in a completely different way to that of my friends. The paralysis, along with the later diagnosis of scoliosis, not only meant I was in a great deal of pain most of the time, but also left me looking and feeling completely abnormal and ill at ease with myself.

I remember spending lots of time in hospital reading women's magazines filled with articles on how to dress for your body type, with advice for hourglass figures, pear-shaped girls and boyish frames. Unsurprisingly they never included advice on how to make your hunchback hot. So I stuck to my baggy clothes to cover my shape and accommodate the brace, in the hope that others wouldn't notice how misshapen my body was. I also rarely wore skirts or shorts, as I didn't want to highlight my super-slim legs. In the world of beauty and fashion, it wasn't as though anyone was being rude about disabled people; we just weren't part of the conversation. To me, that felt worse. It was as if we didn't even exist. That lack of representation had a negative impact on my self-image. I was regularly comparing my disabled body to the perfection of able-bodied models, which I quickly learned was a futile game.

Getting to that point wasn't straightforward; it was a journey. While it was a source of frustration, I think the realisation that I couldn't live up to culture's beauty standards was also what ultimately set me free from worrying about them. What's the point in wasting my time and fixating on something I am powerless to change? There's an old prayer called the Serenity Prayer that says, 'God, grant me the serenity to accept the things I cannot change, the courage to change the things I can, and the wisdom to know the difference.' Regardless of your beliefs, that's just good advice. It was this mindset that eventually set me free to be thankful for the body I have.

Learning to dress my newly disabled body was quite the challenge. I had to consider so many things I had previously never given a second thought to. For starters, I needed to be sure I could put the clothes on and take them off easily. Trying to wrestle into skinny jeans can be a workout for anyone, but even more so from a sitting down position. I'd basically lie on the bed and wriggle around like a worm. On more than one occasion, after peeing in a public toilet, I had to call my mum in for back-up. I was exhausted after thrashing about for ten minutes and needed her yanking assistance.

I also had to be aware of anything that could potentially mark my skin, like seams, studs and zips. These could all lead to pressure sores. I remember being in rehab and seeing that everyone in a wheelchair was dressed in a tracksuit. These were not the height of fashion at the time. I was really fed up. I had always been fashion conscious and this was my worst nightmare. It felt as if my new disability had taken over every aspect of my life, and it was now demanding that I dress like the character Andy from *Little Britain*. I railed against this and decided that I wasn't going to change what I wore just because of practicality. How you dress is a form of self-expression and creativity. I didn't want to relinquish control of that when I had so little control over the rest of my life. I couldn't do anything about being paralysed, but I could choose to look good at the same time.

This defiant attitude paid off a few years later when I was asked to speak to other teenagers who had recently been admitted to hospital with a spinal cord injury. The idea was that, as someone who was a few years down the road living with their disability, I would be able to encourage, give advice and answer questions. I remember one fourteen-year-old girl, who was visibly surprised when she saw me, and immediately blurted out, 'Wow! You're the first fashionable person I've seen in a wheelchair since I came in a few weeks ago!' It was priceless to see the hope in her eyes as she realised she could still dress how she wanted. It seems such a small thing, but we feel so much more confident when we like what we're wearing. It's important to feel you look good. That being said, since becoming a mum I've spent 99% of the time in baggy jumpers, leggings and trainers. I've already locked John into marriage now, and I'm pretty sure slobbiness isn't grounds for divorce.

The mindset shift that took me from self-conscious to self-confident was sparked by a mixture of things. As I grew up I became more self-assured and less worried about what other people thought, and getting surgery to straighten my spine significantly helped. But the single biggest moment that changed everything for me was having an encounter with God at the age of seventeen. I'd been paralysed for four years by that point, and I'd gone camping at a Christian youth festival in the summer with some friends from my church. It wasn't the first time I'd been, so I knew what to expect – late-night chats, grimy shower blocks and a clump of mud in each cup of tea. Every morning and evening there was a main gathering in a huge big-top tent, where we sang worship songs. It was less like church and more like a concert. We also listened to different people give talks from the main stage. It was always a powerful week.

This particular year, it was night three of the festival, and it was announced that we would focus on praying for healing for anyone who wanted it. This usually involved people around you resting their hands on you and joining you to pray for whatever you needed. I usually felt a bit conspicuous at these events, as I could see strangers' eyes dart over to me, eager to pray for my disability to be healed. Many people with a disability have encountered an over-zealous Christian who has been insistent they should pray for them. Although this is often well intentioned it can sometimes make me feel like a project – something that needs to be fixed. It can feel very unloving and unaccepting, despite the intention being the opposite.

A few close friends asked if I wanted prayer, and I said yes because I knew their heart and motives were simply wanting the best for me. They weren't looking for a miracle to happen so they'd have a cool story to tell their friends; they just wanted me to thrive, whatever that looked like. I closed my eyes as they prayed for me, and started to feel a calm presence. A feeling, like burning, came over my body. I felt very emotional, but not being one for public displays of crying, I tried with all my might to stave off the tears. The praying continued for a while and I kept my eyes closed, just trying to focus on God.

All of a sudden someone in the group asked me, 'What's the first thing you'd like to do when you can walk again?' I remember feeling taken aback by the question. It felt like a vulnerable thing for me to admit. I'd never talked about the things I'd missed since becoming paralysed and rarely showed any emotion over it. In that moment I considered not answering the question. I could feel my emotions bubbling up and I blurted out, 'I'd like to dance.' As soon as the words left my mouth, I burst into tears. It was so incredibly cathartic. Afterwards I felt like a new person. It was as if a heavy weight had been lifted from me and in its place I had peace and a confidence I hadn't known before.

I wasn't healed physically, but I loved the way my friend asked the question. I believe that one day God will make all things new again. I believe that there will be no more pain, sickness, suffering or tears – call it heaven if you like. I believe that will be my reality one day – that I will dance.

This reminds me of a quick story I want to tell you. When our son Elijah was five, he found an ornament we'd been given. It was one of a mother and father standing holding a baby, all cuddling one another. He turned to John and said, 'Daddy, who is this on this statue?'

John said, 'Well, we were given that when you were born, so I guess it's supposed to be us.'

Elijah looked thoughtfully at the trinket. Pointing to the tiny model baby he asked, 'Is that me?'

John said, 'Yeah, that's you.'

Then he frowned and continued, 'And is that Mummy and Daddy?'

John said that it was.

To which Elijah replied, 'Hmm… why is Mummy standing up?'

Overhearing the exchange, I interjected and told him, 'It's just an ornament, isn't it? It's not real.'

Still unsatisfied, he proposed a solution to the inaccuracy. 'Hmmm… do you think maybe we should break Mummy's legs off?'

We couldn't contain our laughter at this point, but when we had recovered, John managed to say, 'Oh no! We don't want to break it, do we? It doesn't matter. It's still lovely, isn't it?'

Finally coming to terms with the situation Elijah thoughtfully said, 'Yeah, maybe it can be our statue for when we are in heaven and Mummy can walk again.'

I love the sweet, hopeful purity of children.

When I think about the idea of dancing again, it feels like my happy place. That's why it was the first thing that came out of my mouth that night in prayer at the festival. I grew up loving music and feeling free whenever I danced. Along with my cousin Claudia, I was a card-carrying member of the dance-for-your-relatives-at-every-family-gathering troupe. We made our family sit through many routines to the current hits of the time. Looking back, I cringe at my innocent twelve-year-old moves to far-from-innocent songs. All my relatives were subjected to the performances so frequently that I honestly wouldn't blame my male cousins if they'd been slightly relieved when I became paralysed.

I think one of the biggest breakthroughs during that prayer was knowing that, while much of society treated me as if I was an issue or afterthought, God didn't feel that way about me. My disability wasn't a problem to God. *I* wasn't a problem to God. He still had a plan for my life and if God was OK with me, I could be OK with myself. This realisation changed so much for me. Once you're OK and at ease with yourself, most other people, funnily enough, are pretty at ease with you too. Once you no longer see yourself as a burden, you're far more confident and less likely to minimise yourself or live apologetically.

Goodbye to normal?

Have you ever been through something that robbed you of your 'normal'? If you have, you will know that often the event is just the start. What comes next is often the hardest part, and how you respond shapes your life dramatically. You can't always choose what happens to you. I'm not even sure you can choose your immediate response. There's a cycle of grief to go through before you get to a place of acceptance, and everyone goes through this process at a different rate. But there comes a day when you have to choose to get up, not give up, and recognise you still have hope for a great future.

In my case, it wasn't just my life but my body that dramatically changed too. This left me with the question: 'Who am I now?' My faith helped hugely with this question. It was easy for me to know that my identity was not based on working legs. I believed with all my heart that there was still a plan and a purpose for my life, and being able to walk was not fundamental to that. I was no less Jade for what I had lost. Paralysis stole my legs. I wasn't going to let it steal my identity, my hope or my joy as well.

The same applies for you. Whether you've lost your ability to walk, lost your job, lost a loved one, lost anything else, you are still the same person you always were. Although these big events will undeniably shape you moving forward, how they shape you is an active choice you get to make.

I need to prepare you, though. While I still felt like the same person, when I first received my diagnosis those around me did suddenly define me by what had changed. It can take time and a lot of mental fortitude to fight against the new story or the limitations others put on you. Overnight I became 'wheelchair girl' – and not in a cool superhero way. It was suddenly either all people wanted to talk about or the elephant in the room people desperately avoided acknowledging. I was either the subject of intrigue or an outcast, and it swung like a pendulum from one moment to the next. I could be thrust into the limelight by a group at school who never usually spoke to me, but then snubbed by my friends because they felt awkward around me.

Maybe you've experienced something like this. I'm sorry if you have. It's a tough road to travel. While that may be a part of your story, like it is mine, it isn't the end of the story. You may have to say goodbye to 'normal', but no one interesting is ever described as normal anyway. No one describes the best qualities of their closest friends or their heroes with words like 'normal'.

3

Q: At least things can't get any worse... can they?

A. Well, actually...

John

One of our most viewed videos to date is of me showing Jade a video of another couple. The woman is in a press-up position, her hands on the floor. Her legs are being supported by her male partner, who is holding them up about waist height. If you can't picture it, think wheelbarrow position. The bloke then swings her legs up and flips her body over, and she lands the somersault perfectly. The video then cuts to Jade and me from the shoulders up. I say, 'How good is that?!' Jade replies, 'Yeah', impressed. I then say, 'We should try that!' She voices her displeasure at the idea, I call her boring, then stand up and walk away in a huff, only to reveal she's in a wheelchair.

Of course, you guys saw that coming. But for those who hadn't come across us before, it came as a big shock. The bulk of the response was from people who loved it and, recognising that Jade was in on it, commented on what a great sense of humour she has. We also got the inevitable handful of people who missed the point and wrote things like, 'This is horrible. You can really see the heartbreak on her face as he walks away. If they're a couple, I hope she leaves him.' Additionally, we got a number of comments saying things like, 'She may as well do it. What's the worst that can happen?!' These left me feeling slightly torn. Don't get me wrong, I don't want to assume the worst in people and it's quite a funny joke if the punchline is: 'What's the worst that can happen – she ends up in a wheelchair?' But I do slightly worry that, for some, this may not have been a joke.

I think there are people who believe Jade's life is so bad, it simply can't get any worse. Whereas, compared to others, Jade feels quite fortunate. It's infinitely preferable to be paraplegic than tetraplegic, for example. I think it's harder to lose the use of your hands than the use of your legs. When I broke my leg aged seventeen, the hardest thing wasn't using the crutches to get around; it was trying to hold anything in my hands while I travelled. I'm not saying breaking my leg is the same as disability. All I will say is I had quite a lot of pain and Jade can't even feel her legs. But it's not a competition. Let's not make her feel bad. All experiences are valid.

Jade

People often think that the worst thing about being paralysed is losing the ability to walk, which in reality is much lower down the list of things that suck about an SCI (spinal cord injury). Honestly, one of the things I found the worst was the inability to feel pain in the lower half of my body. This admission usually surprises people. I often get replies along the lines of: 'But surely that's the best thing! I'd love not to feel all the aches and pains in my legs.'

On the one hand I get it – no one likes to feel pain. The avoidance of pain is instinctual. But it turns out that there is a very good reason why God created our bodies to experience pain. It's vital to keeping us alive and healthy. We often don't realise what a great warning signal pain is in our everyday lives to stop us from doing serious harm and irreparable damage to ourselves.

The first time I realised this was when I was eighteen and I was going out for the evening with friends to a house-warming party. It was just down the road from my house, so my friends came over to collect me and we walked (or rolled, in my case) together. As we left, my mum, who was chopping veg at the time, jokingly waved the knife in the air and warned them to bring me back safely. We rolled our eyes, gave a polite laugh and didn't think any more of it.

The street was dimly lit, we were excitedly chatting away as we headed to the party. We crossed the road, but as we got to the other side, I felt a jolt as my friend who was pushing me misjudged the distance to the pavement and crashed my chair into the kerb. The motion flung me forward, out of my chair, and I landed on my hands and knees on the path. My friends rushed to lift me back up and into my chair, and I had to regain my composure after feeling completely dazed and light-headed. As I found my focus and became aware of surroundings, my friends and I quickly checked my legs for any injuries, but they seemed fine, not even a cut or graze, and much to my relief they were bending normally.

We discussed whether or not they should take me home, but I insisted I was fine – a little shocked but fine. We arrived at the house-warming and I got chatting to people. I felt a fair bit better, but still had the odd moment of light-headedness. For the first hour I had trouble focusing on the conversations I was having, and people's voices would suddenly sound very distant, but this soon passed. I felt so normal, in fact, that I decided to round off the night by driving over to a friend's house at 11 p.m. to watch a movie.

While I was there I got out of my wheelchair and sat cross-legged on the sofa. About an hour after I arrived, I started to feel cold. When I asked my friends if anyone else felt the same, I got confused looks and replies of: 'If anything it's too hot in here!' I wrapped myself up with the thick blanket that was on the sofa, but started violently shivering and I could feel my heart racing in my chest. I thought I must be coming down with something, probably flu, so decided to call it a night and head home.

I don't remember much of the drive home. I know it took all my strength to concentrate on the road. I'm shocked that I didn't get pulled over by the police for suspected drink driving, as I'm sure the car swerved all over the road. This would have been particularly bad for me if they asked me to walk in a straight line to prove my sobriety...

Fortunately, I made it home. I went to undress myself but realised I couldn't get my right leg out of my trousers. After a bit of tug-of-war, the trouser leg rolled down and for the first time I could see that my right leg was triple the size of my left. Paralysed people's legs are usually stick thin due to muscle wastage, so the size difference was quite shocking. Something was very wrong.

I shouted up to my parents and asked them to come and take a look at my leg. My dad came downstairs half asleep and turned on the light. I remember the alarmed look on his face when he saw my new thunder thigh. My leg was still bending normally, but there was a huge amount of fluid around the knee and calf area. My dad deduced that it might be a build-up from when I bashed it on the pavement. Although I couldn't feel pain, my body was still trying to tell me that something bad had happened. We decided it would be best to sleep for now, but head to A&E in the morning if it hadn't improved. I didn't sleep a wink that night.

The following morning we went straight to the hospital and took a seat in the waiting room of the busy A&E. One of the perks of being disabled is that even when all the seats are taken, you have your own chair. The doctor decided that I needed an X-ray to see what was going on. We had to wait for hours to get to the top of the X-ray list, as they were extremely busy. At one point my dad even suggested just going home, as the doctor had agreed that it was unlikely to be broken. But we stuck it out and finally I was called into the radiography room and asked to position my leg under the X-ray machine.

After the photo was taken, I could hear the two radiographers behind their screen discussing the images. It didn't thrill me to hear them gasp and for one to say, 'Oh dear, no wonder her leg's swollen; that's quite nasty,' while the other agreed that it would be a long recovery. I wheeled back out into the waiting room and told Dad what I'd overheard. After, yes, you guessed it, more waiting, we were seen by a doctor to discuss my results. He looked slightly sheepish as he admitted that his initial assessment was a far cry from what the X-ray had shown. When I had fallen from my chair I'd sustained a spiral fracture down the entire length of my tibia, which was just being held together by one small piece of bone. Basically, the bone in my leg was so broken that it now looked like a piece of fusilli pasta. The cherry on top – or parmesan, if we're sticking to the same metaphor – was a hairline fracture of my fibula.

To say I was shocked would be an understatement, and I couldn't believe there was so much damage internally, when my leg still moved fairly normally. I told the doctor about my cross-legged movie marathon and he paled. He said that if I could have felt the pain I would have probably passed out. That position would have put direct pressure on the break, and could have caused the small bone holding my leg together to break off completely and skewer my skin. I'm guessing it was no coincidence that that was when I started to feel horrendously ill. My body was basically screaming at me to stop.

Trying to heal a break when you can't feel your legs properly is a complicated process for a few reasons. First, I couldn't be fitted with a traditional cast, because my lack of mobility could cause me to develop pressure sores or skin problems. As I couldn't feel my leg, I wouldn't even know they were developing. So they fitted me with a removable cast that I had to take off for a few hours every day when lying in bed, in order to check if my skin was OK. The cast was bulky and awkward, so I now also needed assistance when transferring in and out of my chair.

Anyone who's broken their leg will know that allowing it to slowly bear weight again encourages it to heal quicker and stronger. This is another thing that wasn't possible for me, so I had to go for an X-ray every other week for two months to ensure I was healing as expected. By my last session I was surprised I wasn't glowing from all the radiation I'd had! I wondered if it might be my super-hero origin story, but to this day my only real power is being able to consume a super-human amount of cake.

This all happened during my A-levels, and because I couldn't risk my leg being knocked at school, I couldn't attend in person until it was sufficiently healed. This was frustrating and isolating for me, as I had to spend every day in my bedroom, on my bed, while trying to do coursework. The friend who had been pushing me when I'd fallen felt really bad about it, but managed to pull himself together enough to go on holiday skiing the very next day. I did jokingly say that the only way to make it fair would be for him to break his leg skiing. I've purposely chosen not to name him, as I think the secret shame he'll have to carry for the rest of his life, knowing he once broke a disabled girl's leg, is punishment enough. So that person shall remain... Sam Cooke.

Throughout my ongoing health struggles, I've been incredibly grateful to my friends who have been there for me. None more so than my Christian friends. I remember after months of being isolated with my leg, Flick, a friend from church, came to my house unannounced and told me she was breaking me out. She helped me into her car very carefully, stretching my leg out on the back seat and then she took me to the beach. We had coffee in the car and chatted and laughed, and it was just what I needed. Little acts of kindness like these have helped me to get through some of the very tough, isolating times in my life.

On another occasion my lack of normal feeling got me into hot water – quite literally. It was the summer holidays of 2011, after my first year of uni. I'd been home for a few days and was keen to catch up with friends I hadn't seen during term time. We'd arranged to meet at the beach to watch the RAF Red Arrows display, and I was rushing to get ready when I noticed that the dress I was planning to wear looked creased. As a student, this wasn't usually a problem for me, but today, for whatever reason, I felt the need to make a little more effort. My mum was out, but I'd managed to find her iron and ironing board and set to work on being a proper adult (some would even say a domestic goddess).

I positioned my chair close to the board, and found to my delight that I could adjust the board's height to allow my legs to fit comfortably underneath. I remember thinking that this ironing malarkey wasn't so hard after all. I even thought I might do it more often! I turned the iron on and waited for it to heat up. I noticed the iron had a fancy button with a puff of air on it that, when pressed, shot an aggressive burst of steam. I found it oddly satisfying. I began ironing the dress, using the steam button a few times for good measure. I was pleased with the job I'd done and went to wheel out from under the board so I could put the dress on.

As I wheeled back, I couldn't believe my eyes. It took a few seconds for my brain to fully comprehend what I was seeing. My bare thighs looked weird and bobbly and my skin had turned an angry red colour. It looked as though the texture of my skin was actually moving, and I was sure I was hallucinating. It was a bit like an optical illusion, or when you get so drunk the room starts spinning – so I'm told. I then realised that my skin was literally bubbling, like lava on a volcano, with blisters forming and popping so fast that I couldn't keep count.

The entire length of both my thighs was cooking before my eyes. I hadn't factored in that the steam effect from the iron would travel through the ironing board. Usually people stand in front of the board when they're ironing rather than have it hovering centimetres above their bare thighs. A shot of adrenaline burst in my chest, and my heart started beating wildly. I tried to form clear thoughts in my head and decide what to do next. I raced out of my bedroom half dressed, and shouted to my dad that I'd had an accident in as calm a voice as I could muster. The calm nature and tone of 'accident' felt like a ridiculous understatement and in no way prepared my dad for the severity of what he was about to see. I sounded more like a child who had just wet herself. As soon as my dad came down the stairs and clapped eyes on my ironed thighs, I saw the sheer panic cross his face. He shouted to ring an ambulance so quickly that the words fell on top of each other. My poor sister, who was twelve at the time, stayed remarkably calm and tried her best to comfort me as my flustered father relayed the accident to the 999 services on the phone.

While we waited for an ambulance, the woman on the 999 call instructed us to put cold water on my legs, but when we attempted to do this it looked as if it was washing off large areas of dead skin from the burn. Unsure of whether this was actually helping, or making it worse, we stopped and nervously waited for the paramedics to arrive. In the wait I felt shell shocked and disorientated. How could something so bad be happening without any warning signals? I also felt guilty for putting my dad and sister through the trauma of it all. My dad in particular always seemed to be around whenever a medical crisis unfolded, and I'm sure the stress has taken years off his life. All I could do was silently pray that my legs weren't as bad as they looked and that from this point on everything would be straightforward at the hospital.

When the paramedics arrived, they immediately wrapped my thighs in cling film and then loaded me into the ambulance. During the journey to the hospital, I asked one of the paramedics why they had applied the cling film, as I wondered if it was to keep the remaining skin on, or to stop potential infection. Funnily enough, I was told it was to protect the nerve endings in my skin from the air, as exposure could cause a lot of pain from the burn site. I didn't have the heart to tell her that, in my case, it was a completely futile attempt to make me more comfortable, and they'd have been better off saving it for their sandwiches. I mean that was the reason I was in this ridiculous predicament in the first place. Did they think I was some sort of masochist? That I was feeling the pain throughout, but just got a kick out of ironing my skin and kept on going?

At the hospital I was seen by a consultant in the specialist burns department. It turned out that I had sustained third degree burns (the worst kind) and that, because the burns were over a large area, I would need an operation to apply skin grafts to the tops of my thighs. Before this could happen all the dead skin, which had now turned a greyish colour, would have to be removed with what looked like a pair of scissors. I had two lovely burns unit nurses do the job as I reclined back on the bed asking them questions. Midway through the procedure I remember one of the nurses abruptly saying, 'I'm so sorry, but this scenario feels really surreal to me. We do this nearly every day, but normally we'd have to sedate or hold down the patient as the pain would be completely unbearable for them. And yet you're lying there quite happily, asking me how long I've worked here!' After a short pause, we all erupted into giggles at how bizarre it all was. I confessed to them that I felt a bit silly for ironing my thighs, but they quickly made me feel better by telling me that at least I had the excuse of not being able to feel. The previous week they had treated a lady with a burn to her chest, as she had tried to iron a crease out of her blouse while still wearing it.

After they'd cut all the dead skin away and bandaged me up, I was admitted onto the burns ward as an in-patient, and I waited to be told when my surgery would be. After a few hours, I started to feel unwell. I was cold and shaky and my heart rate was extremely high. Usually a resting heart rate is around 70 beats per minute, but mine was up at 148. A few friends turned up to see me, but I couldn't concentrate on making conversation as I felt so spaced out. Eventually, I fainted. Thankfully I was already in bed, so there was nowhere for me to fall. If I'd been lying flatter, I wouldn't have passed out, as it's nearly impossible when you're lying down, but I was propped up by pillows and then just sort of sagged into them. It turns out my body had gone into delayed shock after all the trauma I'd sustained from the burn. The nurses had to give me high-strength painkillers to calm my body down. I find it amazing that I could be injured in one part of my body and, even though I couldn't feel the pain locally, my whole body experienced widespread discomfort. Now, whenever I sustain any injury in an area I can't feel, I always take painkillers, as they do still make a difference.

That evening the surgeon came to see me to tell me about the plans for my surgery the following day. He introduced himself and, with a big grin, said, 'Ah, so this is our naked ironing girl!' My face immediately turned bright red and I corrected him. I had not in fact been naked, just not wearing any trousers. I'd obviously been the novelty case that day and the talk of the staffroom. He told me that I should be glad I'd not been wearing any trousers, as I'd have been in a much worse situation. I would have still burnt my legs, but the burnt trouser fibres would have fused to my skin. I wouldn't have realised this straight away and then when I'd next needed to take my trousers off, I would have been taking all the layers of my skin off at the same time. So all things considered, I had the best-case scenario for my type of injury.

At least things can't get any worse… can they?

You're probably thinking that, just like the title of this chapter, at least things couldn't get any worse, but I assure you that things can always get worse. I was put on the burns ward in a bay with six other women. This wasn't unusual, and I tried to hide my disappointment that I didn't get my own room. I always find being in a bay awkward. Your bed is positioned directly opposite a stranger's and unless they are super-chatty and sociable, you keep getting awkward eye contact. The only way to stop this from happening is to have the curtain around your bed pulled right the way round, which feels rude and antisocial. A laptop certainly helps the situation, as you can stick your earphones in and use the screen as a bit of a subtle barrier between you and your opposing bed mate. This was working well for me, but I hadn't anticipated that the woman opposite was about to have a sudden and extreme reaction to the antibiotics she'd been given. Because of the aforementioned earphones, I hadn't heard any warning sounds, so was completely taken by surprise at the noxious smell that hit me like a brick wall. It was so bad that my gag reflex was triggered. I think this moment trained me to deal with my future husband's flatulence, if I'm honest.

I subtly glanced around the room for the culprit. The woman opposite me was bright red and swollen. Target locked. My show had reached the ad break, so I took one earphone out at the perfect moment to hear her let out the biggest, most elongated fart I've ever witnessed, while maintaining eye contact with me the whole time. I looked at her, willing her to laugh so that my imminent outburst would be deemed socially acceptable, but she just sat there. Poker faced. I glanced at the woman in the bed next to Farting Felicity, who was silently laughing so hard her bed was shaking and I quickly realised I couldn't look at her, because Windy Wendy hadn't averted her gaze from me once since she'd become our room's personal air-con machine. Over the next thirty minutes, Gassy Gertrude would let out at least another ten or fifteen stink bombs to the point where the atmosphere was dense and unbearable. Realising I was right by the window, I buzzed for the nurse and requested the window be opened, but to my horror, she told me the windows in the burns unit didn't open, as burns victims needed protecting from the air. No kidding! We all needed protecting from that air! The only saving grace was that, for obvious reasons, fire also wasn't allowed on the burns unit, because honestly, one spark and we'd have all been toast.

That was the cue for all the women with less serious injuries to escape for a walk and fresh air. I, however, was stuck, as I was still waiting for surgery and wasn't well enough to go for a ride. And, just when I thought that was the worst of my troubles, this was when my dinner was served. I couldn't eat any of it, which made me hangry. I wanted to be gracious and kind about the woman, as it wasn't her fault – it's horrible being unwell – but I was so frustrated that I had to share a ward with Trumping Tracy. I was trying to subtly see if I could get moved, or if she could. Thankfully, thirty minutes later, they finally moved her. The stench was so horrendous that after she left, they bagged up her curtain in a hazardous waste bag. I'm not joking.

Skin grafts done, the doctor said the surgery had been successful and I could probably go home the next day with regular returns to check that the skin grafts had taken. They explained that they can fail if the blood supply doesn't connect. In all, it took a few months for my legs to heal. The burns all scabbed over and then I had to gently moisturise the scabs until they peeled off, revealing fresh new skin underneath. On the plus side, it's halved my leg shaving time as no hair grows on my grafts! It's a risky strategy, but if you can face the trauma it does save a few quid on Veet.

Time and time again in my life, just as I think I've faced all I can endure, something else comes along. First the initial diagnosis, then the scoliosis where my rib cage touched my pelvis, then the scoliosis corrective surgery, then more surgery to extend the rods. I've had to endure being told by a doctor: 'There's no funding for your surgery, so you just need to pop pills and shut up, don't you?' (I'm quoting that verbatim, by the way.) I've suffered multiple kinds of medical negligence, including being told by a nurse to shut my newborn baby up when I was hospitalised with a pressure sore as a new mum. So when people say, 'At least things can't get any worse,'

I know first-hand that's not true. Things have and do, and as if all that wasn't enough, I ended up with John. Talk about kicking a woman when she's down!

Rather than my faith being a crutch to lean on when bad things happen, I've found it prepares me to cope well when they inevitably do. The Bible refers to faith as being more like a shield, a protective device that acts as a barrier between us and danger, risk or an unpleasant experience. That doesn't mean that if we have faith we're not going to suffer; it just means it's less likely to harm us in a deadly way. We may live with the traumas and scars, but we are still able to move forward and live with purpose and even joy.

The truth is, much like the fear we discussed in Chapter 1, pain is a good thing sometimes. If we don't feel pain, we aren't always aware of the things that hurt us and we aren't motivated to avoid them. In reality, feeling pain is the warning signal to stop doing whatever it is we're doing. Being numb doesn't stop us from being hurt. In fact, often it leads to more problems. Sometimes it's good to feel the pain of a situation, as it prompts us to distance ourselves. Whether that's from unhealthy friendships or romances, poor financial decisions, reckless thrill-seeking or, in my case, ironing naked.

4

Q: Do you have a thing for disabled women?

A. No, Jade just fell head over wheels in love with me. (Although she says she was just the only one who couldn't run away.)

John

We met when we were both studying at London School of Theology. I remember Jade joining when I was in my second year. My friends and I were looking at pictures of the freshers, and my friend Sam said, 'I'm not sure which one it is, but one of the fit ones is in a wheelchair.' Not in a judgemental way. More out of intrigue.

In the first week, I met Jade for the first time in the laundry room. She was with a friend who was helping her with her clothes. I remember they were all stacked up on her lap and I thought I'd tease her. 'Don't you have a laundry box?' I asked.

'Box?' she shot back.

Crap. I meant basket or even bag. Who has a laundry *box*?

She asked, 'Don't you mean basket?'

I decided to double down. 'No, I guess laundry boxes haven't reached Wales yet.'

This was the first conversation we'd ever had. We hadn't even introduced ourselves or asked each other's names by this point, but I found her fun and sassy. We spoke a bit more and bantered with each other, then I returned to my room, Googled 'laundry boxes' and breathed a sigh of relief when the results confirmed there was such a thing. And then, of course, I DM'd her links to laundry boxes on Facebook Messenger. It wasn't flirty, more just sassy and friendly. I was in a relationship at the time anyway. 'Oh yeah?' I hear you say. 'So how long was it until you ditched her and cracked on with Jade?'

First, don't judge me by your standards, and second, that inter-action wasn't the start of a beautiful love story, as you may be imagining. The truth is, over the next two years while we were at uni together, we barely hung out. We ended up sitting on the same table at lunch sometimes, or when a bunch of students all went to the pub, but we never intentionally met up. We weren't really close at all. It turns out I thought we were better friends than Jade thinks we were. I thought she was a good laugh and fun to hang out with whenever we were in the same group, whereas she thought I was a bit annoying.

It wasn't until I left university that I messaged her one day. It was a friend of mine who actually planted the seed. He knew of Jade but hadn't met her. He'd been at our university before us and left before Jade started, but he reached out to me and said, 'You know Jade Greasley? Could you put the feelers out and see if she'd con-sider going on a date with me?' So I messaged Jade, who politely declined, as she didn't feel she knew him well enough. I didn't then instantly message back with, 'OK then, what about me?' but it's possible it triggered my thoughts later on.

I remember being on holiday in Dubai when I saw a pic of Jade come up on my Facebook timeline and thought 'Whoah!' Her eyes were staring straight down the lens of the camera and she looked incredible. I messaged her something light-hearted and the con-versation flowed from there. I was flirty and cheeky at times, and we got on well.

Then something mortifying happened. I went on what I thought would be a private liking spree of some of her photos. I knew we had a bit of chemistry and I thought that getting eight or nine noti-fications saying 'John Reynolds has liked one of your photos' would make it even more obvious to Jade that I fancied her. The problem was, it didn't make it more obvious to *just* Jade. Unbeknown to me, Facebook had recently changed its timeline. Now, it kindly informed you of your mutual friends' activities as well. So, anyone who was friends with both Jade and me – only about 150 people from our uni – could see on their timeline:

'John Reynolds liked Jade Greasley's photo'
'John Reynolds liked Jade Greasley's photo'
'John Reynolds liked Jade Greasley's photo'
'John Reynolds liked Jade Greasley's photo'
'John Reynolds liked Jade Greasley's photo'
'John Reynolds liked Jade Greasley's photo'
'John Reynolds liked Jade Greasley's photo'
'John Reynolds liked Jade Greasley's photo'
'John Reynolds liked Jade Greasley's photo'
Smooth, eh?

Jade's friend Bethanna was the first to notice, and publicly wrote on my wall: 'Why are you liking all Jade's photos?!' I mean, she could have DM'd me, couldn't she? Mortified, I deleted the comment and then messaged her to explain. I can't remember the exact phrasing, but it was along the lines of, 'We've been chatting a bit. Jade's no doubt head over wheels in love with me by now. PS – I'm not a pervert.' Thankfully, I hadn't liked any of her holiday pics.

I approached dating Jade in the same way I approached dating all women. When I say *all*, I don't want to give the impression there's a list that requires a colon and numbered bullet points; there's only been a handful. But for me, it was just no different. I simply thought, 'I like her – let's see how hard this is going to be.' I know that sounds pessimistic and maybe flies in the face of my usual sunny optimistic outlook on life, but I think it's a reality.

Relationships are hard. All of them. If yours isn't ever difficult, get back to me when you've known each other longer than twenty minutes. It winds me up so much when you watch shows like 'Lust Island' (let's be real here, checking out abs and bikini bods is hardly *The Notebook*, is it?) or *Married at First Sight* and one of the partners says something like, 'I just don't know if they're the one any more. Like, at the start it was all exciting and fun and I got butterflies every time we saw each other, but now the novelty's worn off, I think.'

Now, of course I'm not saying we should all stick with the first person we ever date or overlook big red flags that indicate we're not especially compatible with somebody, but the novelty wearing off is going to be true for every relationship that lasts longer than a few months. I've even heard some people say, 'There must be something wrong with my marriage, because it's not easy right now.' But I think, 'No, that sounds about right.' In fact, that sounds like every relationship in the world ever, at times. Platonic friendships, family dynamics, romantic relationships – they all face hardships. Whenever you have two imperfect people in a relationship, it's going to be difficult. In fact, it's even tough in our relationship sometimes, with only the one imperfect person. And I love that some of you are thinking that's a lovely romantic thing to say about my wife, but some of you know full well who I'm really talking about.

Anyway, when I said, 'Let's see how hard this is going to be', I didn't mean it in a pessimistic sense. It was more: 'I don't want to assume this is going to be too hard for me, when it might not be. So let's see.' It was actually optimism.

On our first date, Jade was amazing at putting me at ease. I remember she was super-confident and natural when it came to telling me how to get her wheelchair out of the boot and how to angle it at her car door so she could transfer into it. She told me the right speed to push her. Apparently, trying to impress her with an all-out sprint was a bit dangerous, and she told me to look out for potholes and uneven pavements, as she'd been tipped out before and broken her leg. No pressure.

We went to Café Rouge and had a steak dinner and chatted loads. It was an amazing night and I knew I wanted another date. I knew this, despite the fact that I had never seen anybody eat olives so bizarrely in my life. We ordered a bowl of green olives to share before our meal and when they came they weren't pitted. For the uncultured reader, that means they've still got stones in them. Obviously, you don't swallow these; you spit them out. Which Jade took literally. It seems that she was so fixated on the idea that you had to spit the stones out that, rather than putting her hand to her mouth and subtly removing the stone, she put her hand in her lap and then essentially dribbled the stone out, so it fell to her palm. Forget her disability, that's the *real* reason I deserve applause for being with her (though Jade has insisted I tell you she'd never done this before and hasn't done it since).

I took her back to her uni, which was the one I'd left a year earlier. We went to her room and watched a show on her laptop. I don't remember which show it was, but I do remember cuddling her and kissing her cheek a few times. I was angling big time. We kept watching the mystery show, but just as I got up to leave, Jade kissed me.

You may think that this is when I tell you it was the perfect end to the perfect night (olives aside), but it wasn't. I've told Jade this already, but it was the worst kiss of my life. I wasn't sure if she was trying to show how much she liked me or to knock me out. The only word I can use to describe it is 'hard'. Not a word you really want associated with your kissing technique. You know those moments in *Tom & Jerry* where Tom gets walloped in the mouth and his lips go to the back of his head and he has to yank his teeth back to the front of his face? Yeah, that was me after I left Jade's room.

I obviously didn't tell her at the time. I mean, I was just buzzing that she wanted a slice. Our subsequent kisses were actually really good, so I didn't need to be, like 'Whoah girl! This isn't a Glasgow kiss'. But we did mention it a few months later and, get this, she thought it was *my* fault, and wondered why I was kissing so hard. Outrageous. I know everyone thinks they're a good kisser but, to quote *How I Met Your Mother*, 'I've got references'. I knew I was, at the very least, passable.

But despite the kiss and the olives, I remember leaving her room that night on cloud nine. She was so amazing – so funny, so great to talk to, so wise – and we had tons in common. For starters, we were both massive fans of sitting down.

The story of our second date went mega-viral on TikTok, with nearly five million views in total. Not at the time, though, as TikTok hadn't even been invented then. If you're a Gen Z reading this, it's true. It wasn't even music.ly or anything – it just wasn't a thing. Most people didn't even have Instagram when Jade and I started dating, which is kind of weird to think about now that social media is my job. Back then I was just a regular Facebook status poster. If you ever want to be humbled, go back through your old Facebook statuses, and when I say *humbled* I mean 'physically sick all over your phone'. (Remember the days of 'John Reynolds is… eating a cheese sandwich and waiting for the bus'? Riveting.)

Anyway, let me tell you the now famous cinema story. I won't use the name of the cinema – not because I'm nervous about a lawsuit or anything; I just can't remember it. As we arrived, I immediately noticed there were stairs at the entrance and no ramp. There weren't loads of steps, about five or six, but when even the presence of a high kerb is a wheelchair user's nemesis, I realised this wasn't ideal. Fortunately, Jade noticed they had one of those mini-platform lifts in the corner. I went to investigate and concluded we needed a member of staff to operate the mobile platform. I went into the foyer and found a teenage cinema employee. 'Hey, I'm with a girl in a wheelchair, so we need to use the lift,' I said.

He looked at me blankly. After a five-second pause he said, 'Yeah.' Another long pause. 'You need a key.'

I frowned. 'Er, yeah. She doesn't come with one, mate, so any chance you could go and have a look?'

Another big pause. It felt as though we were communicating via satellite – like when they have that delay on the news because they're live-linked with Australia. Eventually he said, 'Yeah, sure' and shuffled off to get it.

I hate missing the trailers at the cinema. Yeah, I'm one of those guys. I can also be very impatient, particularly when I feel there is no valid reason to be waiting. After fifteen minutes he finally found the key and came over to help us.

We then joined the queue to get our snacks and drinks, and I moved six grand over from my savings account to make sure I could afford both a fizzy drink and some toffee popcorn. As we got to the front of the queue we went over to the same helpful soul from earlier. Have you seen the sloth scene in *Zootopia*? If you haven't, check it out; it's hilarious and also I think taken from hidden camera footage of our encounter with this employee. By the time he had finished serving us, we were married and Jade was pregnant with Elijah. Eventually, he passed us our tickets for *The Great Gatsby* and said, 'There you go, guys, that's on screen… oh.' He glanced at Jade, and sheepishly said, 'I'm sorry, but *The Great Gatsby* is actually on one of our screens upstairs.'

I said, 'OK, no problem, or is the lift broken?'

He looked even more sheepish before saying, 'What lift?' It turns out the cinema was in a listed building and they hadn't been able to put in a lift due to some laws that protect older buildings from being overly modernised. We'd had no idea about this, however, so there was only one thing for it. I left Jade in the foyer and told her I'd explain the plot to her later. That's a joke. I asked her how she would feel about me carrying her up to the screen. On reflection, I should have asked the guy how far away the screen was first.

We asked if there was anywhere safe to leave Jade's wheelchair in the foyer and we were told they could put it in the staffroom for us. I lifted Jade out of her chair and began to climb the staircase. There were probably thirty or so steps and while Jade wasn't heavy, by the time I reached the top I was struggling. However, being on a very early date, there were two reasons I didn't want her to know that. First, I didn't want her to be paranoid about her weight. And second, I didn't want to come across as weak. So, I pushed through. Once we made it to the top of the stairs, it was then about another fifty yards round the corner to the end screen. Jade opened the doors – good of her to do something, I guess – and in we went. It's important to note here the method of carrying. It was what's known as a 'princess carry'. Think *An Officer and a Gentleman*. Some people online have been confused and assumed I went for the entirely less romantic 'fireman's carry'. As if I slung her over my shoulder like a sack of potatoes.

As we made our entrance, I suddenly became aware of other people and how this must have looked. Because we'd left the wheelchair downstairs, no one else had any context as to why I

Jade (4) in 1994. Evidence that
Jade literally copy and pasted
herself when she had Areli.

Jade (2) with her nan and Josh (1).
If you were wondering where
Areli gets here sassiness from…

Jade (6) at the park. Not *that*
park.

Jade (12) one month before she
became paralysed, with her mum,
Lydia, and sister, Amber (3).

John (6) before Jade had a chance
to influence his dress sense.

John's (7) first day at junior
school.

Jade's thirteenth birthday in
hospital. This was the moment her
'cake for breakfast' habit began.

Jade (13) in the hydrotherapy
pool hoist.

Jade (13) and her dad, Mark. The floatation noodle for her legs was overkill.

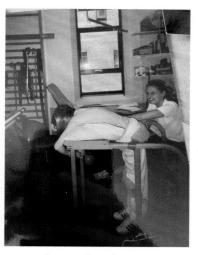

In the standing frame (aka 'the torture device') with Jade's physiotherapist, Nesta (2003).

X-ray of the metal work in Jade's spine to straighten her scoliosis (2007).

Jade's first holiday in a wheelchair (2004). TripAdvisor review: 'Couldn't go on most of the rides, 2/10.'

John and Jade at London School of Theology, with friends Sam and Bethanna, before the romance blossomed (2012).

Jade's graduation, three months after they started dating (2013).

© Gabby Lewis

Engagement shoot in Mumbles, Swansea, by Jade's BFF and future maid of honour, Gabby Lewis (2015).

Live action Dubai engagement shoot (2014).

Admiring the ring by the
Burj Khalifa, Dubai (2014).

Jade's bridal entrance with her
dad, Mark (26 September 2015).

Swansea Bay doing its best
impression of Barbados.

Gorgeous and stunning… and
Jade.

© Mark Tatton

John giving his groom speech.

John and Jade at a family wedding (2015).

© Luke Aylen

Welcoming Elijah into the world (2016).

© Luke Aylen

Mumma and Elijah.

Beautiful Elijah.

Welcoming Areli with her proud big brother (2019).

Snuggly sass bucket with her lion (Areli means 'Lion of God').

John with our little cartoon boy and sleepy newborn.

Areli's first day out.

Christmas Day walk (2021).

At our church, St Luke's Blackburn (2022).

Strong girls' club on our accessible adventure weekend at Calvert Lakes (2023).

was carrying her. I could see men looking at me, like, 'Who's this under-the-thumb bloke giving us a bad name?' And then the women looking at me as if it was the cutest thing they'd ever seen and elbowing their partner with, 'Why do you never treat *me* like a princess any more?'

The reality is, it wasn't romantic. It was just practical, and even though I said exactly that on TikTok, there are still comments like, 'Not romantic?! Sir, you are the personification of romance! So many men would have just left.' While that might be how some people have experienced dating (e.g. 'My date wouldn't even walk me to the bus stop, let alone carry me up a flight of stairs'), I think you have to be especially cold hearted to just shrug when someone disabled needs your help. Not only that, but we'd also already got the tickets and we wanted to see the film. So it was the obvious thing to do. Anyway, I carried her up a couple more steps to our seats, popped her into hers and went back down to grab the drinks and snacks… and my inhaler.

At the end of the film, we waited for everyone else to leave first. The last thing I wanted was to try to navigate the hustle and bustle of everyone leaving, and get knocked down the stairs. For one thing, if I became paralysed too, Jade would definitely leave me because she's a shallower person than I am. We waited for everyone else to vacate the screen and then I stood up and got ready to carry her back downstairs to her wheelchair in the foyer. I noticed three older ladies at the back of the cinema still slowly making their way down, but I didn't think they'd be any trouble. And if anything did kick off, I reckoned I could take them. I picked Jade up and we made our way downstairs. Now, I don't know if these ladies were a bit giddy from seeing Leonardo DiCaprio on the big screen, or if they'd snuck some gin in with their lemon and barley squash, but they started shouting things out like unruly teens at the back of the school bus. 'And they say romance is dead!' bellowed one. '*That's* the Great Gatsby!' yelled another. If you've read the book (or, like me, seen the film), you'll know that doesn't even make sense. As I say – giddy. But then one of them starting singing Bonnie Tyler's 'I Need a Hero'. Jade and I were cracking up as I carried her down, which made the already challenging job of carrying her a lot harder.

Without the wheelchair visible for reference, there was no reason these ladies could have known why I was carrying Jade, so she decided to be a little mean. As we got to the bottom of the stairs, we went round the corner to Jade's chair. I popped her down and then pushed her out to the front doors to leave. As we passed the old ladies, she just looked at them and shook her head disapprovingly. They nearly choked on their false teeth. If you follow us on social media and have ever wondered where our younger child, Areli, gets her sassiness from, I think you now know. I have no idea what happened after that, but I like to imagine them swearing each other to secrecy: 'Margaret, we don't breathe a word of this to anyone, all right? Deidre, not even the girls at bingo. We take this to the grave with us, you understand?!'

Jade

You probably want to know how we got engaged. If you don't, tough. Why did you buy the book?

We went to visit John's uncle and auntie in Dubai and, unbeknown to me, while we were out there John bought my engagement ring. I later found out he'd already asked my parents for their blessing during a trip to Bristol Zoo, while I was in the toilet. My mum immediately said no, completely straight-faced. Thankfully she was joking, and they gave their permission. I had no idea what had taken place when I returned from the loo. All I could think about was how annoyed I was that the person in front of me took ages and then stunk it out. Sadly, the lavatory dramas would only continue in Dubai.

Before we get to the engagement story, which has its own restroom-related melodrama, let me tell you another from that trip. We went out with a group of people one evening for a roast dinner and drinks. About an hour into the evening, I needed to use the bathroom. The restaurant was in a complex and didn't have its own toilets, but customers could go through the double doors to the adjoining gym and use theirs.

John and I ventured through the doors to find them, where the man on reception looked panicked and told me, 'The restroom is over there, but I need to call Fatima first.' I was confused, as I could literally see the toilets, and I said, 'It's OK, I can go by myself.' But he insisted and phoned for this Fatima woman, saying, 'Fatima will chaperone you in the ladies' toilets.' I told him I wouldn't need any assistance and went off by myself as John returned to our friends. I went into the bathroom stall and just as I began my wee, I was aware of feet so close outside the cubicle they were poking underneath the door. It gave me a bit of stage fright, to be honest, but I assumed it was Fatima.

When I'd finished, I came out of the cubicle and Fatima was there, staring at me. Silently. Like in a horror film. I was perplexed. I went over to the sink and washed my hands as Fatima walked over to monitor my hand-washing too. I have no idea whether she thought she was helping or just overseeing. Was this Emirati hospitality, or was I going to get a mark out of ten? It was all very confusing and to be honest I couldn't get out of there quickly enough.

Just as I was about to go back and tell John about the weird situation, I opened the door to find the man from the reception desk on his knees before me, presenting me with a Twix multipack in his outstretched hands. He looked up at me and said, 'I apologise, Madam. This is for going to toilet by yourself.' Apparently solo wees were deserving of confectionery. I returned to the table and recounted the story, much to everyone's bemusement and orders of, 'Get back there for round two, so we can save on dessert!'

Anyway, a few days later John told me he was off to look at patio furniture with his uncle, which sounded a suitably masculine thing to do together, so I neither questioned it nor fancied joining them. In actual fact, he was going to buy me a ring.

John

When we got back from buying the ring, I knew immediately where to store it. I didn't want to keep it on me, as Dubai is hot and shorts aren't the best place to hide a ring box. I didn't want people asking, 'Is that a ring box in your pocket or are you just semi-pleased to see me?' So I'd come up with an ingenious plan. I hid the ring in the tool compartment of Jade's wheelchair. For those who don't know, under the seat of most wheelchairs is a tool compartment. It's sewn in on the underside and then Velcro attaches it to the wheelchair user's cushion. If I needed to get Jade's tools out at any point and 'fix her chair', I'd have to crouch down or, I don't know, get down on one knee, move her legs out of the way, pull apart the Velcro and *voila*! It was the perfect crime.

Jade

I obviously had no idea that I was basically my own ring mule. It's very rare that I get my tools out and if I do get a puncture or need something adjusting on my chair, I tend to get someone else to do it. The Queen didn't service her own chariot, did she? I have to credit John – it was a pretty clever plan.

The day of the engagement came and I still had no idea. We'd decided to go out for a full English breakfast at a golf club in the morning, which was really nice, and then John told me he wanted me to experience a posh afternoon tea as well, so we did that later. By the time the evening came and he told me he'd booked a restaurant for a steak dinner near the world's tallest building, the Burj Khalifa, so we could see the fountains, I still wasn't suspicious – we were in Dubai! We'd done lots of nice things that holiday, but I was very full. I tried to put him off. 'Why don't we do it another night?' I suggested. But he insisted, so I thought I'd just eat something small.

I was a bit annoyed that before we left he asked me if I was going to have my hair up in a pony tail all evening. I looked at him quizzically, and more than a little offended replied: 'Yes. Why?' And he told me, 'Oh, I just think it might look nicer down, that's all.' What? I was really annoyed. I told him I was going to wear my hair however I wanted and, as it was hot and humid, I was going to wear it up. It really surprised me, because he'd never said anything like that before. It didn't feel controlling, as I knew he wasn't like that, but I felt he was being unnecessarily opinionated. I now know that he was actually being really sweet. He's super non-confrontational usually, so he would probably have hated even mentioning it, but he wanted me to be happy with how I looked in the engagement pictures. Thankfully, I was. What can I say? I can pull off many looks!

We had an amazing meal at the steak house, although I could tell that John was a bit distracted. Once we'd finished, we headed out to watch the fountains at the foot of the Burj Khalifa. On the way, I told John I needed to use the toilet and he said he would go and try to find a cash machine while he waited. I later discovered he went off to scope out where we needed to stand by the fountains so that his uncle and friend could get photos of us when he proposed. Looking back, he put so much thought into it. He'd even paid for me to have my nails done the day before, so they looked good for ring pictures. He's a sweet boy really.

The bathrooms in Dubai are rarely in the restaurants themselves. Most of the places we ate at were in malls anyway, so you have to use the mall toilets when you're dining. On our way to the fountains I found a bathroom. I was wearing a playsuit that day and as you will know if you've ever worn one, there is no easy access when it comes to using the toilet. The entire playsuit has to come off. I got undressed and, just as I was mid-wee, a male cleaner using a radar key opened the toilet door and walked in to put his mop back in the corner of the toilet. I screamed as what felt like the entire mall looked in on me sitting on the toilet in my underwear. The man just froze and then, unbelievably, continued to put his mop back! 'CLOSE THE DOOR!' I yelled. He fumbled his words and backed out and closed the door. I was horrified. When I'd finished and was reunited with John, I told him what had just happened. Was he outraged? Was he angry? Was he upset for me? If he was, he didn't show it. He simply responded, 'Oh, that's weird,' in that I'm-not-really-listening way men do. I now know why he was so distracted; his mind was totally elsewhere as he tried to get me to the perfect photo point.

John

My plan was to get Jade to the predetermined spot where my uncle and his friend were hidden and could take a photo with the fountain show in the background as I proposed. The fountain shows are incredible, with the water seemingly dancing in time to songs like 'Billie Jean'. Once the show was in motion, I was going to make an excuse about there being something wrong with Jade's chair and move her back, get down on one knee to get her 'tools' out of the tool compartment and then pull out the ring box, before asking her to marry me.

Jade

Obviously, I didn't know any of this. So when John said one of the brakes on my wheels wasn't working properly and he was going to fix it there and then, I told him not to be ridiculous. I was thinking, 'For goodness' sake, you've rushed our steak and then hurried us to the fountains, and now we're finally here, you're going to start haphazardly fixing my chair mid-show?' I protested, but when he grabbed my chair and wheeled me back abruptly about two minutes later, I honestly thought he'd got heat stroke. He was acting so weirdly. He spun me around, knelt down, spread my legs widely and started rooting through my tool compartment. This isn't a euphemism, but in a strict Muslim country with a very high view of modesty, I was starting to get worried. Just as I was about to plead with John to get up, he pulled out a random tiny box and said, 'What's this?'

I was confused. I'd never seen it before in my life. What was it, and why was it in my wheelchair? A few moments later, the penny dropped. I looked up at John and could see him smiling. I don't remember exactly what he said, but he told me he loved me and wanted to spend his life with me, and then he asked me to marry him. There's a photo included in the centrefold that perfectly sums up my reaction. My hand is over my mouth in total shock.

I said yes and we hugged, then John's uncle Pete and his friend Brad came out from their hiding places and got more pictures of us. We then went up to a bar where Pete's wife Emma was waiting and we celebrated together.

John

To say that Jade is not a gushy person is an understatement. I wouldn't say she's closed off, as she does get emotional, but she's not as effusive as I am. However, immediately after the proposal she couldn't stop talking. To be fair, with all the food, toilet dramas, fountain fiasco and then getting engaged, that's pretty understandable. She kept saying she just had no idea. Job done. Smashed it. I remember as we travelled back to my uncle's I kept seeing her glancing at the ring, and it melted my heart. I was half delighted, as I thought it was probably a good sign, but half nervous too. I hoped she liked it, but was slightly paranoid she might be looking at it, thinking, 'I'm pleased I'm engaged, but what the hell is?' I kept thinking she deserved a bigger diamond, but I'd done my best with what I could afford.

In general, our life together has been met with love and acceptance from our friends and both sides of the family. I think that may have contributed to my surprise when we started receiving so many questions from social media followers as our platform started to grow.

I have been asked on more than one occasion on social media if I have a thing for disabled women. It surprises me every time. I try to be careful not to clumsily label all awkwardness as ableism – some people probably don't mean it that way – but whether it's overt or internalised, it's still a weird question. Sure, it would have some validity if I had four exes and all of them were wheelchair users – and Jade would definitely be worried! But Jade is the only disabled person I've dated. Nobody asks me if I have a thing for blondes because she's blonde, or a thing for people who can't speak properly because of her Welsh accent.

I've even had people say things like, 'You could have had any woman. Why did you choose Jade?' Which I find hilarious and heartbreaking in equal measure. The notion that I could have had *any* woman is the funny bit. Although, I have to say, Jade found it a little funnier than was polite. Yet the idea that if only I had known I could have had any woman then I wouldn't have chosen Jade, makes me realise how widespread the negative perceptions of disabled people are. Jade is the best partner I could ever have asked for and that remains true whether I could have any woman or not. I didn't get stuck with her. It's not some sort of pity, charity thing. She was and is and will always be my top choice. And besides, isn't the fact that we all have other options, yet we choose to be with the one we're with, what makes relationships so beautiful, and what makes romance so, well… romantic?

I sometimes find these questions depressing and indicative of the tendency towards commodification of people, even within personal relationships. I don't believe this consumeristic approach towards dating will ever make us happy. There is no such thing as 'upgrading' your relationship. People aren't phones. Sure, someone might be better suited to you, but half of that compatibility, or lack thereof, is on you. I've heard some self-centred people talk about their new partner as an upgrade on their last, which is usually a way of lashing out at an ex. Sometimes this is in response to poor treatment, but other times it's just because their previous partner wanted to keep them accountable for their actions and their new one is more willing to put up with their toxicity.

Jade

Many disabled people find themselves caught between two equally undesirable statuses. We're either fetishised or infantilised, which can make it hard to find our place in the dating world. I think the fact that John gets asked this question online is evidence of both of these. 'Do you have a thing for disabled women?' might imply that, for some, we're a kink. Or maybe it's seen as a challenge, or a novelty conquest for the body count. Maybe it's because we're just so undesirable that we're simply a hilarious anecdote following a round of the game Never Have I Ever. 'NO WAY! A disabled chick?!'

Do you have a thing for disabled women?

Journalist and wheelchair user Lucy Webster shared an email thread of her correspondence with the dating website Matchmakers on X (formerly Twitter).[1] When she made it known she was a wheelchair user, she was told that, unfortunately, 'Matchmakers Dating is not a specialist agency' and 'Regretfully, others are not always open to dating someone living with your disability… so we have found that achieving good outcomes for full-time wheelchair user clients can be quite challenging.'

Even when disabled people put themselves out there for love, they may receive messages rooted in the assumption that their disability is intrinsically undesirable. Disabled people are already more than aware of the prejudices in society and that many people may not consider them as a romantic option, but can you imagine a dating app singling out other people because of perceived 'undesirable' factors? Substitute 'full-time wheelchair user' for ugly, overweight or unemployed, and imagine the level of media attention such an email would get.

I think it's also possible that the question 'Do you have a thing for disabled women?' is not asked with sexual intrigue or curiosity, but from a place of surprise. 'Seriously? I mean *can* she even? *Should* she even? Should *he* even?' As if this is – or worse, I am – something taboo.

At one stage this would have hurt me, but I'm long past that now. I know that at best it's curiosity and at worst it says more about the one asking the question than about me. I think if I'd been in the modern dating world of Tinder and the other apps, I would have found it extremely hard and probably would have experienced more rejection and ableism. I don't think I would have had the guts to turn up to a date without the person I was meeting already knowing that I was in a wheelchair. But that provides its own challenges surrounding perversion and safety too, so I feel for those with disabilities navigating an online dating space.

---

1   L. Webster, X, 10 February 2021: https://twitter.com/Lucy_Webster_/status/135948971061643
6736 (accessed 12 March 2024).

Thankfully, although we get asked odd questions online, our friends, family and people who know us well aren't surprised by our relationship and never have been. They understand that John's caring character and willingness to love me as I am is totally fitting with who he is, and they know that my patient character and willingness to overlook just how incredibly annoying he can be is just what I'm like. We all have our crosses to bear.

5

Q: Is your husband your carer?

A. Are you joking? He can barely look after himself.

John

Last year we went on an ITV gameshow – me, Jade, my mum Julie, Jade's mum Lydia and my sister Katie. We won't spoil it for you, as you might want to check it out on catch-up. We had the best time and loved the TV presenter, who was hilarious, but even he fell into the trap many of us can when it comes to interabled relationships. At one point he asked me in a segment that didn't make it into the final show, 'So, John, did you know Jade before she needed to use a wheelchair?'

I replied, 'No, we met at university and she was already disabled.'

The presenter gave me a huge hug and said, 'This man is the most amazing man in the world. Wow! You are such a good man.'

And the audience clapped. I was slightly surprised, and between Jade and myself we just made a few jokes about how she had to put up with far more from me.

But it's odd, isn't it? I mean, we all understand on one level that romantic relationships require sacrifice. So in a relationship where one person is incapacitated in some way, it makes sense that there may be an even greater sacrifice from the other person, at least physically, and that is to be admired. That part I'm fine with. What makes me uncomfortable is the implication that Jade is somehow damaged goods and it's surprising that someone could love her. At its root, that line of thinking is objectification and materialism. Of course it's only natural to want a partner you find attractive and to enjoy and celebrate their beauty, but I do. Jade's gorgeous. She's not a competition winner! I always find it odd that some people think I must be an incredible person simply because I'm married to a woman who cannot walk. Behind closed doors you have no idea what actually goes on. I might be a scumbag. What about all the Dutch ovens I give her, for example?

Of course, many go the other way too. In their desire to elevate those with disabilities, they can clumsily slip into wokeness. While well meant, comments like 'There's nothing wrong with your wife' can have the opposite effect, downplaying all she's been through and the challenges she faces every day. I realise there is a good heart behind these messages and they are probably a way of saying that she's still worthy of love and dignity and still has value. But the phrase 'There's nothing wrong with your wife' sounds perilously close to a Tory disability benefits policy. It's hard not to be sarcastic sometimes, but I often want to reply, and sometimes do, 'Seriously? There isn't? She made me carry her up steps last week when the lift was broken. So lazy!'

Jade

I remember watching a documentary where Kate Garraway spoke about her husband's health deterioration after he contracted Covid. He became so unwell he needed carers, and Kate remarked on some of the advice and comments from friends and family who had said things like, 'You can leave him, you know. You didn't sign up for this.' She would reply, 'Pardon? I made vows. I literally did sign up for this.' Sure, we hope that we have more 'better' than 'worse' times, and more 'health' than 'sickness', in our marriages, but promises are promises and should mean something.

You only have to watch dating shows from over the last ten years to know that a consumeristic attitude towards dating and marriage has emerged. As we've already discussed, the multitude of these programmes has normalised the idea that the second the butterflies are no longer there, you shouldn't be either.

I recently saw an Instagram video showing Brené Brown discussing the shared roles in a marriage. She said:

> Marriage is never fifty-fifty. Sometimes he's on twenty... I got [him]... other times, I've got ten and he's at twenty and we know that we have to sit down at the table and have a conversation any time we're at less than a hundred combined and figure out a plan of kindness towards one another. A partnership works when you can carry their twenty or they can carry your twenty.[1]

I think many people would assume that John is mostly carrying my twenty, and while my additional health challenges mean he probably carries more than I'm able to, there are many times where the opposite is true. Most weeks there are also days when I'm carrying his twenty.

I'll be honest, it does frustrate me when people think John's primary role in our lives is to serve as my carer. Don't get me wrong, there have been times when John has had to care for me when I've been very ill, but that isn't true of our entire relationship. Most of the time we're just like any other married couple. I'm fairly independent and can take care of myself, especially at home where everything is accessible. I don't just look after myself, but I'm also able to look after my children without help. The outside world is a whole other story, though, and I regularly need help to get around in a world not designed with wheelchair users in mind. I've had amazing friends who have had to carry me upstairs, help me shower and wheel me across all sorts of difficult and sometimes dangerous terrains, just so I won't miss out on life experiences because of my disability.

Since being married that mantle has passed to John and he's absolutely brilliant at supporting me. I had no say in becoming paralysed and having to face all the challenges that come with it. For John, it was a choice to share in my struggles because of his love for me. I think that's such a credit to him, but it's also what we do when we love someone. We choose to share in their pain. Their battles become our battles. That's real love, and I know that's

---

1 https://www.tiktok.com/@timferriss/video/7241204908203003142 (accessed 12 March 2024).

probably what people are acknowledging when they gush about what a great guy John is. The problem for me is when people fail to realise that this sentiment goes both ways. Just as John helps me with struggles relating to my disability, I help him with his struggles relating to his ADHD.

John

In March 2023, I found out I had attention deficit hyperactivity disorder (ADHD). It's an odd diagnosis to come to terms with. It's not life-threatening or even life-changing. Technically nothing changes at all, as it's a genetic condition you're born with it. However, it still forces you to reflect on what you've been through.

ADHD is part of the neurodivergent family and means your brain hasn't developed in a neurologically typical way. Without being too scientific about it, those with ADHD have lower levels of the neurotransmitter dopamine than those who are neurotypical. This is one of the 'feel good' chemicals that are released in the brain, and it plays a role in pleasure, motivation and learning.

Whenever we do something pleasurable, dopamine is released into our system, we feel good and that motivates us to do more of that thing. It's what's called our reward system and it plays a crucial role in driving behaviour. Various things can release dopamine into your system, but they tend to be things that are novel, interesting, challenging or urgent.

That's one of the reasons we don't all find the same things fun. If I've done something a million times and you've never done it, it's less interesting to me because it's lost its novelty. Whereas for you, it's more enjoyable. If I find something really interesting but you find it boring, then I'll get a dopamine hit from it and you won't. If I find something challenging but you could do it in your sleep, I'll probably enjoy it more than you. Or if I need to complete a project in an hour but you still have until the end of the month, I'll be more motivated to work than you.

Those with ADHD produce dopamine at a lower level, so they are chemically wired to seek more as a result. It's why ADHDers can struggle to focus, can forget things that don't give them a boost, can be late, can leave things till the last minute, can be impulsive and pleasure-seeking.

Inevitably, this leads to challenges within relationships. I tend to get on best with people who are the perfect balance between entertaining and good at listening. I talk a *lot*. I interrupt a *lot*. I'm incredibly disorganised and flit between tasks. I struggle to prioritise important things. I'm forgetful. I'm often late. This can be frustrating for friends and family – and for me. There isn't enough space in this book to go into every way it impacts me and why, so I'll save it for the sequel. That is, if I can muster the attention span to write another book.

For a long time, I thought this was an issue with my character. I thought I was weak and immature. Whenever I let people down, be it at work or home, I thought I just needed to grow up. Let's face it, struggling to do things you don't find interesting sounds incredibly juvenile and selfish, doesn't it? So I would be really hard on myself. I'd tell myself I needed to up my game and I'd resolve to be better in the future. But then it would happen all over again. And again. It felt as though no matter how hard I tried, some things were just unbelievably difficult for me, near impossible at times. I wondered if it was depression or anxiety. Why were there some days when I was an unstoppable force, and some when I just couldn't get going? It was confusing and demoralising when I was at a low point.

I think it took me a long time to get the diagnosis because I wasn't the naughty kid at school. In the late 90s, early 00s, the general perception of kids with ADHD was that they couldn't sit down for more than five minutes, they'd be incredibly disruptive in class and they'd throw at least one chair at a teacher per lesson before storming out shouting, 'It's not my fault, sir; it's my ADHD!' Whereas I always did pretty well at school. I don't say this to brag, but I sat on the back table in primary school. I know, right? Clever *and* well behaved. I passed my 11+ and went to Tunbridge Wells Grammar School for Boys, and mostly I loved school, if I'm honest. I look back on it with fond memories, so there weren't loads of very obvious signs of any neurodivergence.

The hyperactivity I experienced manifested itself through talkativeness. I was mentally hyperactive as opposed to physically. Although I'd fiddle a lot in class with my pen, or I'd doodle, I was always listening. In fact, I've now learned that this fiddling is called stimming, short for stimulating. It's thought to be a way of self-soothing and providing little regular dopamine boosts to prevent ADHDers becoming overwhelmed. The constant changing of lessons provided novelty throughout the day, doing well provided a challenge, playing sport in PE and being creative in music and art provided things I found interesting. School wasn't too hard for me personally.

That is, until I got to my GCSEs, the national exams we all had to sit at the age of sixteen. When it came to self-driven learning, I fell off a cliff. Not literally. It wasn't an orienteering tragedy on my Duke of Edinburgh scheme. I just couldn't motivate myself. Revision? You mean going over the same stuff I've already learned, *again*? Doesn't sound as if there's much dopamine to be found there. No thanks! If you need me, I'll be winning the treble with Tottenham on Football Manager 2005.

So, much to everyone's surprise, I didn't get especially good grades. It wasn't a total disaster, but I didn't fulfil my potential. I remember coming out to tell my mum and I looked at her and said disappointedly, 'I didn't get any As.' I thought she might be cross, but she was smiling. Then she laughed and I realised she thought I was joking. 'Come on, how many did you really get?' Uh oh. My usually incredibly charming and hilarious pranking and teasing was coming back to bite me. 'No, I'm not joking. I really didn't get any.' She wasn't cross, but I knew she was disappointed.

A-levels at eighteen didn't go much better for me and I think, for a while, the agreed narrative was that I had just stopped working when I turned fifteen. Of course, as you grow up you do find other interests. I'd heard rumours of girls, for example. They sounded cool. But it wasn't that. It was that I'm not a very good self-starter. I need accountability and deadlines, and as I got older those became increasingly my own responsibility.

You may be thinking that a lot of the symptoms and experiences I've mentioned above fit everybody, and to some extent you'd be right. We're all dopamine-dependent creatures – it's how we're made. There will probably be some overlap for you too. Does that mean everyone is a little bit ADHD? Well, no. For example, we all need sugar, but that doesn't make everyone a little bit diabetic, does it? Those with type 1 diabetes have low levels of blood sugar, and as such need it more than someone without diabetes. So too with dopamine and ADHD.

It was Jade who first mentioned to me the possibility that I had ADHD. She'd seen content on social media that reminded her of me. I'm always slightly wary when she tags me in something with a comment saying, 'This is so you.' It's never some popular guy at a dinner party, wooing the whole table with his hilarious stories and affable charm. It's usually something criticising how long I take to poo, how I'm not very good at receiving criticism or some other targeted character assassination designed to communicate how much she's grown to despise me (I guess she's right about me not taking criticism well).

I watched the ADHD video and replied, 'Yeah, but that's everyone!' I wasn't out and about, by the way. We were just doing that classic thing millennial married couples do, where we message each other from different rooms in the same house. She called out from another room, 'It's not me!' So I went to chat to her face to face – like old-fashioned people do.

We talked about it, watched some more videos on ADHD together and in that time it was honestly a little like the scales had fallen from my eyes. I started to look into it more deeply and, of the twelve big indicators of ADHD that I found, I had eleven.

I booked a test. The NHS waiting list was more than a year. This was insane given how difficult it is for people with ADHD to actually book a doctor's appointment and fill in the forms. I thought if I could only get that done, I'd probably go straight to the top of the list. Thankfully, we'd started making a bit of money through TikTok and we felt it was important to try to understand this as soon as possible, as I was struggling profoundly both at work and at home. Together, we agreed to book a private assessment.

I cried when I was officially diagnosed. Not because I was sad, but because I was relieved. I finally had an explanation for the struggles I'd had throughout life. I felt a sense of vindication. I wasn't simply pathetic or weak or immature; there was a reason I struggled and it wasn't my fault.

Since my diagnosis I have obviously been milking it for all its worth. Need me to do stuff that's not exciting? Soz, Jade – ADHD! Need me to wash the dishes? But what about my ADHD? Need me to stop playing PS5? Sorry, did you forget I have ADHD? Want me to mow the grass? Sorry, I've got hay fever, babes. And also ADHD.

Of course, I'm joking. I do find all those things difficult, but I'm working hard at not weaponising my diagnosis. In fact, joking aside, that is also part of the struggle. When you are an ambitious person who doesn't want to look back on life regretting missed opportunities or failed potential, yet you struggle with executive function, how do you know when you need to simply try harder, and when you need to be kinder to yourself? It's similar for those with a mental health illness, a disability or any condition that leaves them with good days and bad days. When do you push through and when do you rest? Interestingly, while our struggles are different, this is an area where Jade and I can really relate to each other. We both know what it's like to go to bed with plans to attack the following day with a positive and productive mindset, but then wake up in the morning to find your body just says, 'Not today.' It's helped us to empathise with each other and ask the right questions, because we know a little of what it's like.

I honestly think that in our various struggles Jade and I are close to being perfect for each other. I'm not her carer, but I'm very caring. I like to be useful and to help people. I get a buzz from it (dopamine, baby!). Similarly, Jade is the perfect balance of good at listening, *incredibly* patient and genuinely hilarious and entertaining, so for most of our marriage we get along like a house on fire – just without the loss of belongings, tragedy and threat to life. (I've never understood that metaphor, to be honest.)

Regarding Jade's disability, I have never once resented her for it. However, there are times when we share frustration. There have been moments when I've been working full time and Jade has been at home with a small child – one of ours, usually – and she's desperately wanting to go out to the shops and buy some food and get some fresh air and a change of scenery, but the logistics of driving and a wheelchair and pram are just too difficult to navigate alone. That means she ends up stuck in the house all day, and then after a long day at work I have to go out to the shops and then mess up every item on the grocery list Jade has given me. I don't *have* to do the latter, it just always seems to happen that way.

Jade

We need each other. No one is completely self-sufficient. The notion of 'self-made' millionaires is a myth. While hard work, guile and a lot of luck may help us make a success of ourselves, we'd be lying if we didn't acknowledge all the people who help us along our journey towards our goals. The concept of self-sufficiency is a soothing lie our culture tells us in a bid to help us feel powerful when we feel weak. The problem is, deep down we know it's a lie, so that sense of power is fleeting and the frustration with our weakness inevitably returns, often more powerfully than before.

I think both John and I appreciate the love and care we show each other. Neither of us is the other's 'care worker', but we both need each other's regular support and help. Isn't that the way in every relationship and marriage? At least sometimes?

One thing I've tried to improve on over the years is swallowing my pride and asking for help. When I was younger, probably through fear of putting people out, I was really bad at asking for help when I needed it. I would have rather not gone to an event than feel I was being a nuisance. But as I've got older, I've recognised we all need help sometimes. The single mum doesn't get a social life if she never asks people to have her kids for her from time to time. The teenager who doesn't drive but has a Saturday job in the middle of nowhere is unable to work without their parental taxi service. The recently widowed pensioner is unable to do some of the practical jobs her husband used to take care of without the support of a kind neighbour. The list goes on. We need each other, and asking for help is often an opportunity to show strength and build friendships, not a sign of weakness or inadequacy. We are made with our unique gifts and strengths, but we mustn't embrace individualism to the degree that we lose the community and relationships we were created for.

6

Q: How have you had kids?

A. Well, when a mummy and daddy love each other very much…

John

In 2022 there was a TikTok trend where people would share 'Questions people have asked me about [insert their unique situation here]'. Usually, those questions were direct and rude. For example, the woman who shared 'Questions people have asked me as a mother of five children' listed: 'Don't you think you should stop now?', 'Why don't you use contraception?' and 'Don't you own a TV?' The creator would then refuse to answer any of the questions and instead just dance to Alexis Jordan's song 'Happiness' in a carefree manner. The trend was an 'up yours' to nosy people with presumptuous or invasive questions.

I joined the trend with my own video, 'Questions I'm asked about having a disabled wife'. It went viral on TikTok, Instagram and Facebook, with more than 18.5 million views across the three platforms. The five questions I shared were: 'Can you have sex?', 'Can she actually be a good mum, though?', 'Can you guys have sex?', 'Do you have a thing for disabled women?' and 'What about sex?' These are all real questions I've been asked.

The three most common comments were: 'Wow, bro's got moves' (fact), 'Why are people so rude?! Who would ask these questions?' and (the most common of all) 'Why aren't you answering the questions?! We need answers!'

Jade

It probably won't surprise you to hear that at university I was asked on more than one occasion whether I was able to have sex. People often fumbled their way around the question, usually euphemistically, with questions like 'Are you able to have kids?' I'd always answer that I'd been told I could.

On the whole, this question came from men. Sometimes it felt like genuine intrigue and was asked gently and politely after a level of friendship had formed. I think they saw me cracking on with life, being able to do most things, having a good sense of humour and being like every other girl at uni, so to them it was just a natural question from one friend to another. Other times, it felt like a bit of a clumsy chat-up line or a way of testing the waters to see if I was an option.

Online, people are much more blunt. The questions 'What about sex tho?', 'Can she even feel it?' and 'How have you had kids?' are all commonplace. In person, the questions about sex mostly stopped when I got married. I think people just assumed we must be able to. A man might be able to overlook my disability, but signing up for a sexless marriage felt less likely. Plus, once I got pregnant, I think people mostly worked it out for themselves. However, since our social media presence has taken off, I've been confronted with the question all over again. People feel emboldened from behind a keyboard to ask the questions they really want answers to.

Sometimes I find myself torn. On the one hand, I don't owe people the answers to their questions. People aren't entitled to have their curiosity sated, no matter how inquisitive they are. On the other hand, I want to bring awareness to the fact that our culture often infantilises disabled people, with the assumptions that they can't have sex, don't want to have sex or can't enjoy it if they do.

For a start, every disability is different, and every person with a spinal cord injury will be affected differently. Not to mention the big differences between the anatomies of disabled men and women. So I cannot speak on behalf of the entire disabled community. People seem to want me to reveal once and for all whether those with spinal cord injuries can even feel sex. That's a question I just can't answer on behalf of everyone. Some can, some can't.

Behind the question is the motivation for asking it, and that matters. Let's be honest, not everyone is asking for wholesome reasons. Some who ask claim to do so because they want 'educating', but why do any of us *need* educating on a couple's favourite sex positions? (Yes, I've been asked. No, I didn't answer.) All this shows that the fetishisation of disabled people is very real. The fact that John has been asked if he has a thing for disabled women, as we've seen in Chapter 4, is yet another demonstration of my point.

In my late teens and early twenties I would go out with friends to bars and clubs. Initially I rarely got romantic attention, but suddenly I started having men throw themselves at me. Some would try to wheel me off before my friends could intervene, some would just kiss me without my consent. One guy literally slid across the dance floor on his knees so he could be the same height as me, and just knelt there, waiting to kiss me. I sat there ignoring him, feeling uncomfortable. He eventually passed me a piece of paper with his number on it and left. I immediately put it in the bin. Don't worry, just like his chat-up lines, it was recycled.

Most people recognise that I'm just a regular woman. They understand that because sex is a physical activity and my disability comes with physical limitations, it may be difficult at times. Because of this, it's not unusual to assume that the sexual area of life isn't a reality for us, but decreased physical ability doesn't inevitably lead to diminished sexual desire. Just because someone might find it hard to cook doesn't mean they don't like to eat, does it?

I didn't think of the sexual side of my life a whole lot in my teens. I realise I'm probably unique in that regard. Don't get me wrong, I had the odd 'I wonder if I will get married' thought, but for a big chunk of that period of my life I was very unwell and almost always in survival mode.

The first time I thought about it was as a fourteen-year-old. I had to go to the National Spinal Injuries Centre at Stoke Mandeville for rehabilitation. Before that, I'd had a lengthy stay in a regular hospital since it first happened, but not received any specialist care yet. I went for a two-week stay at Stoke Mandeville for a kind of full-body MOT. It was like a boot camp where I was taught life skills again so I could live as independently as possible with my disability. As well as teaching me how to get up kerbs, dress myself and cook while in a wheelchair, they also included a session on sexual health as part of the course.

As I was under sixteen at the time, I didn't attend any of the more comprehensive sex seminars, but I overheard conversations among some of the older patients. I remember being surprised and fascinated that even people with a higher injury level than mine, sometimes even being paralysed from the neck down, were being encouraged and supported to explore their sexuality. At one point two nurses came to talk to me about sex. Usually that would have been sexual health care but, given my age, it wasn't applicable. Instead, they spoke briefly about my future, and it was the first time that sex had even been referenced. I remember them saying, 'You're probably wondering if you can have kids? You can! You're probably wondering if you can have sex? You can! Your fertility isn't affected at all. People with spinal injuries can still enjoy sex and have a fulfilling sex life.' I felt embarrassed and instantly wanted to move the conversation on. I *hadn't* been wondering about any of that stuff and at the time I didn't really care.

Many of the other people at the centre were older than me. Plenty were already married or in long-term relationships by the time they had their injury, so relearning and rediscovering their sex life in their new situation was a crucial part of keeping their relationships strong. I imagine that would have been very tough to navigate at times, going from an able-bodied sex life to one with more limitations. The comparison and frustration at what they had before would be difficult to overcome. In that regard I was thankful that I had nothing to compare it to. My only experience of love on top was the song by Beyoncé.

I quickly noticed that romantic relationships were one of the hardest aspects of life to navigate post-injury. That's probably because the dynamic of the relationship would naturally shift and perhaps stop feeling equal, particularly in the early days. I saw quite a few relationships of fellow SCI patients break up because they couldn't handle the new reality they were now living. In some cases the abled-bodied partner felt overwhelmed by all the challenges that a new disability brought. In others, they were pushed away by the person with the SCI because maintaining a romantic relationship on top of everything else they were going through was too much. No matter the cause, I couldn't help but notice that the couples where the woman was disabled and the man was able-bodied had a much higher likelihood of failing than if the roles were reversed.

This was disheartening to see and made me wonder whether men were more shallow than women. On the other hand, it was so encouraging to see the couples that did stay together post-injury; the depth of love they had for one another was enviable. They were always the same couples who were laughing and bantering together through all the challenges they faced.

My injury was something that I knew any future partner would have to consider when dating me, but it wasn't the defining factor of my life by that point. I didn't want or need a carer, but I knew I'd need somebody who was caring. I think my physical limitations caused me to be more reserved than many of my friends and more reserved than I may otherwise have been if I hadn't become paralysed. Some may think I missed out, but I actually have the perspective that this caution saved me from making unwise decisions. As teenagers, we often make decisions based on whether something is fun or not, and on the here and now, without considering the long term. Looking back, I think it saved me a lot of time and energy. It certainly helped me swerve the bad boys. Pun completely intended.

So, in answer to the question you're all asking – or at least if you're not, TikTok is – to be honest, I don't know whether our sex life is normal. I've only had sex as a disabled woman and what even is 'normal'? But can I have sex? Yes. Do I enjoy sex? Yes. Does the disabled Karma Sutra contain fewer positions? Probably.

I'm sorry if this, ironically, is anticlimactic for you. If you were hoping to hear wild stories involving sex swings, then I'm going to have to disappoint you – we don't own one. But if you happen to know anyone who wants to gift us one… I'm joking, that's a joke. Especially if it's second hand.

John

When I reflect on why, from my perspective, Jade and I have managed to maintain a healthy marriage and sex life over the years, I think it's because we're on the same page about the big things in life. We waited until marriage to have sex. No, seriously, we did. That one isn't a joke. Of course, it wasn't easy. Especially for Jade. I mean… hello? Have you *seen* me? What discipline that woman has!

I want to choose my words especially carefully in this part, because there is zero judgement from us on those who don't wait for marriage. Our waiting was intrinsically linked to our faith and I'm of the opinion that Christians shouldn't expect those who aren't Christian to live by their Christian standard. I wouldn't have waited if my faith wasn't a central part of my life. But I will share with you the reasons why we waited – not in a bid to try to persuade you to do the same, but with the hope that it at least makes sense to you why many people who have a faith opt for this.

The biggest motivation was that my faith teaches me to try to put other people's wants and needs ahead of my own. Of course, I fail at this a lot of the time. I know in my heart that the whole world doesn't revolve around me, but from where my eyes are, it kind of looks like it does. So I often live as though it does. It's not great, but it's part of our imperfect human nature. We all know the world would be a better place if everyone lived selfless lives, but the reality is we'd like other people to make the world a better place by living *their* lives selflessly, while we consume and gratify ourselves with anything and everything we desire.

Many of us make the mistake of thinking that true freedom is found in being able to do what we want, when we want, with whomever we want. And yet, too often, that way of thinking and living leads to more pain than joy and more captivity than freedom. We think too short-term and end up a slave to our desires, using people along the way. It is said that people were made to be loved and objects made to be used but somewhere along the line we've confused the two. I love that saying – it is so true.

How does this relate to waiting until marriage to have sex? Well, I wanted Jade to know that I loved her for more than her physical attractiveness and for more than simply what she had to offer me. I wanted her to know I wasn't using her. I wanted her to know I would still be there tomorrow; that I was in this for love, not just lust.

Let's face it, sex can be confusing. I don't mean the mechanics – I think I've figured those out. But it can make you *feel* a lot of things, and that's by design. I believe God made sex, not as a free-for-all to enjoy with as many different people as possible before your shagging days are behind you, but for a committed relationship. Whenever you're intimate with someone, especially sexually and when you orgasm, you release a chemical called oxytocin also known as 'the love hormone'. It plays a crucial role in bonding you more closely with the person you're being intimate with. It's very hard for 'no strings attached' to remain that way when your very design is fighting against it. Your very being is actually fighting *for* attachment.

Regardless of your views on sex, I don't know a single person on the planet who wishes their long-term partner or spouse had had more sexual partners before they met. I don't know any wife who says, 'I just wish my husband had slept with more women before we got married,' or a husband who says, 'I really wish my wife had had a higher body count before we got together.' I also don't know of anyone who likes to be used or would be happy if someone they loved were used by another person. Yet, when we reduce sex to a skin-on-skin physical activity based on instinctive desire, and we forget about the emotional and spiritual side of the connection, it's inevitable we will use people or be used by people.

I remember seeing disabled activist Sophie Morgan post on Instagram[1] about the time she discovered she was a meme. A

---

[1] https://www.instagram.com/p/C3Wgz1ALjGK/?hl=en&img_index=1 (accessed 12 March 2024).

picture of her sitting in her wheelchair was being circulated with the caption: 'Women are like parking spaces. Normally all the good ones are taken, so sometimes when nobody is looking you have to stick it in a disabled one!' It's difficult to concisely analyse everything that is offensive about that joke. The sense of entitlement to sex and another person's body, the rape culture, the low view of disabled people – it is staggering really, and understandably heartbreaking for Sophie and disabled women (if not all women) everywhere.

While waiting had challenges of its own, it did help us both to know that neither of us was simply using the other. Jade knew she wasn't some fetish for me, and I knew Jade wasn't just using me like some gorgeous, hunky piece of meat. Shut up. Why are you laughing? It could have happened.

Given what we've said about the the human condition and our natural urge to act in our own self-interest, it should come as no surprise that sex is another area where we can be deeply selfish. We want our needs met without necessarily caring about what the other person wants in that moment. Porn doesn't help with this. No one watches porn hoping to satisfy anyone but themselves, and when we enter a relationship having trained ourselves to get what we want, when we want it, we quickly find that isn't the reality of real human interactions. The porn industry would be bankrupt if it told the truth. No one ever has a headache on Pornhub, but when we get married we realise headaches, periods, tiredness, children, illness and all manner of things mean that it's hardly 'sex on tap'.

Jade

Given my health record, it probably won't surprise you to hear that illness has got in the way of our sex life at times. I don't mean the classic 'pretend you've got a headache because you can't be bothered tonight' excuse. I think that's wrong. Besides, if you're going to use your health to get out of it, you need to properly commit. That's why I've tended to opt for the 'genuinely life-threatening illness' excuse. I find partners are a lot more receptive to hearing 'not tonight, love' when you've been hospitalised.

When Elijah was four months old I developed a pressure sore without realising. The pregnancy had been relatively straight-forward for both myself and Elijah, and after having a C-section I was sent home to start my life as a mother. I thought we'd made it through the worst and it would just be a case of adjusting to motherhood.

I decided to visit my mum in my hometown of Swansea. I was feeling the exhaustion and mild hysteria that comes with not sleeping for three months straight, but overall I was coping OK. On the second day there, I woke up with the tell-tale signs of an infection: headachey, fatigued, lack of appetite and just a general unwellness. As a paraplegic I'm particularly prone to urine infections, so I know the signs well and just assumed that was the source. I made an appointment to see the GP and expected to be sent home with antibiotics. The doctor requested I do a urine sample that he could test there and then. When the results came back negative for an infection I remember being really confused. I had all the usual symptoms and I knew that there was definitely something wrong with me. The doctor prescribed me antibiotics anyway to see if they would help.

Back at my parents' house I decided to have a shower while my mum watched Elijah, to see if that would help me feel better. Afterwards I saw that the towel I had been sitting on had a small blood stain on it. I sighed, thinking I'd probably scraped myself while transferring in and out of my chair. When you have an SCI you're encouraged to check your body every day, and in particular your skin for any signs of injury that may have happened without you realising it, especially in places you can't see easily. In the bubble of new motherhood, I hadn't been as diligent in checking myself recently. To my surprise, when I got my compact mirror out to check behind me, I saw an angry red patch that looked like a graze, just where my upper thigh met my left buttock. It didn't look great, but it didn't look awful either. I concluded that this must be the site of infection that was making me feel unwell.

I showed my mum and she agreed that we should get it looked at by a doctor. By this point it was early evening and the surgery was closed, so we had to attend the out-of-hours service at the local hospital. The doctor I saw diagnosed me with a deep infection of the skin, called cellulitis, caused by bacteria. I didn't know how the infection had started and the doctor didn't seem to have any conclusive ideas either. I was sent home with different antibiotics. I was relieved that the source of my infection had been discovered and really hoped I'd start to feel better soon.

The following day I felt worse, but assumed the antibiotics hadn't had enough time to kick in. I continued looking after Elijah with my mum's help, but I started to find things like breastfeeding harder as I felt more and more unwell.

That evening my mum went upstairs to her bedroom, and I stayed downstairs with Elijah in my old room. I was sharing the double bed with him, as it was easier to breastfeed him in the night without having to get up, particularly given how poorly I'd been feeling. I'd taken my antibiotic, but I threw it straight back up, which was obviously concerning and meant I wasn't getting the medication my body needed. That night things went from bad to worse. My temperature skyrocketed, which brought on a fever. I couldn't keep any food down and I felt delirious. I remember having a revelation in those midnight hours about the power of motherhood and the unbreakable bond between a mother and child as, although I felt so unbelievably unwell, I still managed to nurse and look after my baby, making sure all his basic needs were met. Before becoming a mother, there was no way I'd have been able to think about looking after anyone else in the state I was in.

By the morning my mum was getting increasingly worried, and I remember feeling panicked that I was so dehydrated and couldn't produce any milk. Especially as, up until that point, Elijah had been exclusively breastfed and on the few occasions we had tried him with a bottle, he had completely refused to drink from it. This fact, along with my drastically deteriorating health, led my mum to call the GP again to get an appointment for that day, but much to her dismay they couldn't see me until five o'clock, which was still hours away.

After the phone call to the GP, my mum's friend Hayley popped over to drop something off for my mum. As soon as she saw me and heard about my symptoms, she offered to take me straight to hospital, as she suspected I had sepsis. By this point I was barely able to pass urine because I was so dehydrated and I had a serious case of brain fog. We arrived at A&E and, after explaining the situation, the receptionist told us to take a seat and wait to be seen. Hayley pleaded for me to be seen straight away as she had nearly lost a friend to sepsis a few years before and knew that time was of the essence when treating it, but nobody seemed to see the urgency. After an hour of waiting, with my condition deteriorating further, I was struggling to answer simple questions. Hayley demanded for me to be seen immediately and would not leave the reception desk until they agreed.

A nurse took a blood sample to get an indication of infection. If you have more than seven indicators in your blood, it's likely you have an infection. My result came back with more than 144. I was immediately given IV antibiotics, and fluids for my dehydration, as the doctor confirmed I had sepsis. I remember being concerned for Elijah, worrying that the infection could cross over into him from my milk. I was relieved when they told me that breastmilk is naturally antibacterial.

Thankfully I responded to the IV antibiotics quickly and started to feel better by that evening. The consultant came to assess the site of my infection, which now looked very angry, swollen and hot to the touch. It was thought likely to be a grade 4 pressure sore (the worst kind), which had been caused during my pregnancy by the extra weight I'd been carrying, and it had become infected. For those who don't know, pressure sores are wounds that develop when constant pressure or friction on one area of the body damages the skin. This stops blood from flowing normally, so the cells die and the skin breaks down. It's a common issue for people with paralysis, as we are sitting down in one position for most of the time, and usually we don't feel them developing. I hadn't had one before, so I didn't know how to recognise them.

The hospital team said that they would have to surgically remove all the infected tissue and leave me with an open wound that would have to be packed and dressed until it was completely healed. They warned me it would be a slow recovery, as the hole they were going to leave in my leg would be quite big. I had the surgery the very next day and finally saw how big the wound was. It was 5 cm long and 2 cm wide, in what looked like an eye shape. Plus it was 4.5 cm deep. They packed it with an absorbent dressing and told me to stay off it as much as possible to aid the healing. Considering it was near my bottom and I spend 100% of my waking hours sitting, that was a very hard thing to do. My only option for staying off it was to lie down on my side, on either a bed or a sofa. They initially told me it would take about six weeks to heal, which at the time felt like an age. It meant I couldn't do the four-hour journey back to my home in London and would have to stay at my parents' for all that time, with a nurse coming out to dress the wound daily.

An additional challenge of having an open wound is that they're very wet, and constantly ooze wound exudate. This is very unpleasant and often quickly soaks through dressings. This can cause the wound packing to fall out, and meant we had to call for a community nurse numerous times a day. When this happened, it left me bed-bound and stressed, because the wound wasn't properly covered.

Weeks went by and there was no improvement, so I had to be readmitted to hospital a few times with further infections. All this, while caring for my then-four-month-old, was horrendous. I felt completely exhausted from infections and drained from sepsis, plus I was sleep deprived from doing the night feeds with Elijah. John was still working back in London, but would make a mad dash to Swansea at the weekend to see us, but it wasn't enough, and I missed him terribly. After six weeks my wound showed no sign of healing and I decided I needed to go back home to London and have my care transferred there. It was a risk to do the journey, but by that point I was completely fed up and needed to be in my own home.

After being back home in London for two weeks I deteriorated once again and was rushed into hospital during the early hours of the morning. I had sepsis *again*. My wound was looking worse than ever. I was seen by a specialist tissue viability nurse, who audibly gasped when she inspected my wound for the first time. She suspected that the infection was now in my pelvic bone and I would need an emergency MRI for confirmation. She was visibly angry at the state my wound had been allowed to get into. She raised a safeguarding concern, which meant my care would have to be investigated for medical negligence.

The MRI results confirmed that the infection was in the bone, which meant drilling into it to release the infection. Following this operation, my wound was 7 cm deep, which meant a longer healing time and I had to go on IV antibiotics to clear the infection. It was mid-December and I desperately wanted to be home for Elijah's first Christmas. The only way for that to happen was for John to learn to administer my IV antibiotics at home, which the hospital wasn't very keen on. After many conversations we managed to convince them that we were responsible adults, and John didn't have a life insurance policy out on me.

The first problem we encountered at home was that we didn't have anywhere to hang my IV bag. They'd sent us home with all the medical supplies necessary to administer my antibiotics for the next few weeks but no IV stand. This was a problem, as all IV bags must be hung above the patient's heart, otherwise there isn't enough pressure for the IV fluid to infuse. Ever the problem solvers, we found that hanging my IV bag from the light fittings in our bedroom and living room worked just as well, although it did look a bit odd when we had visitors over. I also had the very real fear that John might kill me. Obviously, I mean accidentally, but I did get very paranoid about him checking for air bubbles when setting up my IV line. I had survived too much to get taken out by a bit of rogue air.

My recovery took months, during which I had to spend 99% of my time lying on my side, being visited by nurses every day to change my dressing, and managing to entertain baby Elijah all by myself while John was at work. I had no family living close by and a few friends who had to work themselves, which meant being housebound was incredibly isolating.

Being a new mum is hard for anyone, but especially when you're ill and can't leave the house to go to any baby groups or even just grab a coffee and some fresh air. It was mentally tough, and I felt I was in survival mode most of the time. I was being looked after by an amazing tissue viability team, who would encourage me to keep going and do all the work I needed to get better. There's so much that goes into healing a chronic wound. I had to eat well, rest well, have the right type of dressing and not put any pressure on the wound by sitting on it. The latter was by far the hardest part, as it meant I was so limited in what I could do. From start to finish it took me fifteen months to heal fully, and twelve of those months were spent at home, only leaving the house a handful of times for hospital appointments.

That was probably one of the only periods of my life when I couldn't find any humour. Neither at the time nor looking back. Finding joy was hard, and I want to be real about that. With other incidents, my body went through trauma but my heart didn't. With sepsis, my whole being experienced that trauma. Previously, I'd had close friends nearby to help me, and while I'd made some friends in London, they hadn't had the time to become deep relationships. I felt incredibly lonely. Trauma is tough. Isolated trauma is horrendous.

The second year of our marriage was made up of many nurse visits to clean and treat my wound, constant monitoring of my health and, despite spending the whole year in bed, very little sex. John and I had waited for two-and-a-half years while dating to sleep with each other, and one year into marriage we had to take another year off. (Which, John insists, is the equivalent of seven years in 'man years'.)

John

I think that waiting until we were married before having sex gave us the best chance of forming a healthy relationship. We knew the sexual attraction was there. Once you have that attraction it's important to see if there's more than just physical desire. Could you be good friends? Does the other person have a character you admire? Do you share similar beliefs on the big, important, non-negotiables in life? Could you be a partnership for life? Because I've got news for you – there are no hot eighty-year-olds. I've already reached my peak and I'm thirty-five. There will always be someone better-looking (I'm aware of at least three men who are hotter than me). I'm on my way down now.

I believe the waiting set us up perfectly with the best chance of surviving the year-two drought. That might seem extreme, but remember we had a newborn too, and I was working full time and looking after my sick wife. Looking back, it was brutal. I know that most relationships struggle a little when the days of being solely lovers and friends are behind you and you enter that new chapter of life when you form a parental alliance to fight against the tyrannical rule of your offspring. But it wasn't just our children we had to face.

So, in summary, that's how we had kids; the good old-fashioned sexual way. Whenever I'm doing a youth talk on sex I like to refer to it as a bumpy love cuddle, because it always gets a wonderful reaction. A mixture of laughter, incredulity and cringing. But I'd like to think we can be more mature here. We banged. Get it? Great.

7

Q: Wasn't it a bit selfish of you to have kids?

A. Yes, kids are very easy to have around, and we only had them for cheap labour. It was either that or get a help dog.

John

I remember vividly when I first knew Jade was pregnant. I didn't know it scientifically, just intuitively. We were watching *The Blacklist* and the main female character, who is a spy, discovers her partner is also a spy who's been sent to spy on her. Obviously this throws the validity of their whole marriage into question. She ties him up and threatens to kill him for being a double agent. As Jade and I were watching this, I glanced over at her to see her glaring at me. No blinking. It still gives me shivers, thinking about it. Nervously I said, 'Are you all right?' And she said, 'I'd do that to you. I'd do that to you if I had to.' Then she nodded towards the scene on the telly. I laughed, hoping it was a joke, but slightly worried it wasn't. She faintly smiled. To this day, I'm not sure if the smile was confirmation she was joking, or in response to her imagining me tied up, begging for my life.

That moment, as well as a few other uncharacteristically emotional and angry episodes that week, made me suggest a pregnancy test. Obviously I didn't know how Jade would be when she was pregnant, but this was like her time of the month x 100. She'd flit between intense feelings of anger with ridiculous threats (which we both laughed at a lot when the anger subsided) to tears and overwhelming emotions. One day Dick Van Dyke was on the UK TV show *This Morning*. He was still dancing at almost ninety years old and Jade broke down in tears. When I asked what was wrong, she blubbed, 'I just love that he's still doing what he loves, even though he's nearly ninety!' It was clear to me that she'd either lost her mind or was with child. I immediately went out and bought a pregnancy test. We'd been married just eleven weeks by this time and it was a big surprise, although obviously one of the best surprises we've ever had. #Virile.

Jade

Being pregnant was quite hard for me, especially towards the end, with the extra weight from the baby pulling on my stomach. It made transferring from my chair to the sofa, bed, toilet or shower a real workout every time. Having to get up in the middle of the night whenever the baby is on your bladder is also more challenging if you're in a wheelchair. Most people shuffle to the toilet in a half-asleep state, but for me, I had to focus on getting into and out of my chair without falling on the floor. The bump itself also made life hard. If you've been pregnant, you'll know how difficult it is to bend over, even if you can stand. If you can't stand, it's like sitting down with a basketball up your top. Even if I drop things now, it can be an effort to lean over and pick them up, but with a bump it just wasn't possible. John spent his whole life collecting things for me from the floor.

John

Jade went into hospital during her thirty-sixth week of pregnancy in order to be monitored because, for some reason, women with a spinal cord injury are more likely to go into labour early. If that didn't happen, the plan was to have a C-section around the thirty-eighth week. I'd gone in to stay with her for the first night. Jade had her own room with an ensuite – shower *and* bath – at Stoke Mandeville's maternity ward. I was sleeping on a Z-bed on the floor, while Jade for some reason got the comfy adjustable bed with the TV, fan and room service… sorry, 'call the nurse' bell.

Ever since we'd arrived, I'd been eyeing up the bath. We didn't have one at home, as we'd needed to convert our bathroom into a wet room and there wasn't space to have both a shower and a bath, so it had been a while since I'd sat in my own warm, soapy filth. Earlier in the day, I'd remarked to Jade, 'It's cool we've got a bath.' She didn't even look up from her magazine as she said, 'You're not having one.'

This might seem pretty controlling of her, but there was no door between the bathroom and her room. It was essentially all open-plan. There were curtains separating the rooms, but they didn't meet in the middle, because there was a metal runner along the ceiling for a hoist. So if the patient was unable to walk, and maybe even unable to use her wheelchair or transfer herself with the extra weight of pregnancy, she could be helped into the hoist and then transported from her bed to the bathroom. This meant that me having a bath wouldn't be a particularly private affair. Anyone who came into the room would be able to see me through the gap in the curtain.

It got to 6 p.m. and I pondered in an off-hand way, 'Do you think any nurses or doctors will come by at this time?'

She instantly replied, 'You're not having a bath, mate.' How did she know?

At 8 p.m. I said to Jade, 'Surely no nurses will be coming in at this time.' I'm not entirely sure where I got the idea that there would be downtime in a facility with twenty-four-hour care. They don't clock off at 5 p.m. and leave you to fend for yourself through the night, but for some reason it seemed unlikely to me that anyone would come in. 'I'm going to have a bath,' I confidently asserted.

'Don't have a bath, John.'

'I'm going to have a bath.'

'Do not have a bath.'

So there I was… in the bath, reclining in the steamy paradise, bubbles up to my shoulders, candles lit, reading my Kindle, 'sounds of the rainforest' playlist on, rubber duck bobbing laps round the tub. Bliss. OK, I might not have had half that stuff, but it was genuinely very relaxing.

What I hadn't realised was that the lights in the bathroom were on a motion-sensor, so about ten minutes into my relaxing soak, the lights clicked off. At first, I thought this was going to be annoying, but then I realised it just added to the ambience. The light from the main room – where Jade was in the bed – poured through the two-foot gap in the curtains and became the perfect relaxing mood lighting. It felt like I was in a spa.

About two minutes after the lights had gone off, a nurse came into the room to do Jade's observations. I froze completely still. I didn't dare to look over, because the only thing worse than unexpectedly seeing a naked man in a bath is unexpectedly seeing a naked man in a bath who is staring at you. As she continued monitoring Jade, I gradually realised that she didn't actually know I was in there. While she was lit up by the ceiling light in the room with Jade, I was in relative darkness. She hadn't noticed me. I was then hit with the fear that even the slightest shift of my body weight or a poorly timed fart might set the light sensors off again and suddenly the room would be illuminated, revealing my naked, now pruney, body. Then I'd look like some sort of twilight hospital creeper. Hiding in the shadows, totally nude, waiting to ruin a medical professional's day.

Thankfully, I managed to stay still enough and, while I'm sure she fully observed Jade, she didn't observe me. I was safe. That being said, no amount of bubble bath was going to bring back the relaxation now. I blew out the candles, paused the sounds of the rainforest and even completely removed the Father Christmas bubble beard. The moment had passed.

I raced to wash my hair as quickly as possible and was just about to get out when suddenly Jade exclaimed, 'Oh no!'

My mind jumped to worry for her and the baby. I called through, 'Are you OK? What's wrong?'

She replied, 'I've just accidentally pressed the wrong button. I tried to switch channels on the TV and I pressed the call button instead.'

Despite her protestations, I'm still convinced to this day she did it to get back at me for having a bath against her wishes. She maintains otherwise, but I think she was secretly seething that I'd had a near nude encounter with a nurse and got away with it. Or perhaps she got confused and was trying to put *Call the Midwife* on the TV. Either way, seconds later the same nurse came back into the room. This time I was lit up like Las Vegas, and even now I'm still unsure why I said this, but as she looked over at me and shot me a confused smirk, I said, 'I'm just having a bath.' As if what was really weird about this situation was the lack of clarity about what was going on.

Obviously nothing could take the shine off becoming a dad, but the following day every time a new doctor or nurse came in to talk with Jade and see how she was doing, I couldn't help but look at them closely to see if there was a slight smile. I'd bet my house on the fact that the nurse told everyone all about it. 'You know Jade in room 12? I just walked in on her husband having a public bath. Like this is some sort of hotel.' I tried to put the whole thing behind me, although Jade wasn't so keen to stop mentioning it.

The following day, I left her in the hospital to go into work. I had been helping my team at church as they cleaned and reorganised the youth room. Just as we finished, Jade called me and said, 'I think my waters have broken!'

I said, 'What do you mean "think"?'

She replied, 'Well, the midwives aren't 100% sure, but they're saying you should come back in.'

I couldn't drive at the time, so I called our friend Charlotte, who very kindly dropped me at the hospital.

Jade

We had a clear birthing plan. I was going in early to be monitored, and if I went into labour I'd have a Caesarean-section there and then. (I wonder if Caesar would have been happy if he knew he was mostly going to be associated with salads and sunroof births.) If not, we had a scheduled date booked for two weeks later. However, my usual consultant wasn't in, so I had someone I hadn't met before, who for some reason was desperate to ignore my notes and 'explore our options'. She kept pushing me for a natural birth, saying things like, 'Just because your spinal cord is injured, the human body is still remarkable at automatically giving birth. You may not feel it, but it doesn't mean your body won't be able to. Women in comas have given birth.' I kept pushing back, saying, 'I don't care. I'm not going to experiment with this. We have a plan, and I want to stick to it.' I don't know why she was so keen to avoid a C-section. Part of me wonders if it was cheaper not to do the operation, or if she wanted to have on her CV that she'd been part of a paralysed woman's natural birth. I'll never know, but it was all very strange.

By the time John arrived, I was feeling upset and stressed. It was a relief to see him and know I had some back-up. It took John, our surgeon and the spinal nurse putting their collective feet down, and me getting emotional, to finally convince the consultant to back down. She left in a bit of a huff. Thankfully we had an amazing surgeon, who really supported us and apparently had a huge show-down with the consultant. The surgeon came back in ten minutes later, clearly frustrated, but put our minds at rest, saying, 'I won't let her deviate from the plan, because you could go into autonomic dysreflexia.' This is a dangerous syndrome involving an overreaction of the nervous system. It's most common in people with spinal cord injuries and is a kind of alternative to the body's response to pain. It's the same 'shock' I went into when I broke my leg and burnt my thighs. She then assured us, 'You don't have to worry. I will be performing your C-section myself.'

The rods in my spine meant I wasn't able to have an epidural, so I was fully anaesthetised for both my C-sections (that's for my two children, not just a botched first attempt). This meant John wasn't allowed to be in the room and I wasn't awake. While not unheard of, it was a strange experience for John to be waiting outside, with no idea what was going on, and then to be handed a baby. It was equally bizarre for me to come round and be presented with my child.

I am so thankful for the various medical teams at Stoke Mandeville hospital for all their love and support in my life. Without that hospital I might not even be alive, and I certainly wouldn't have had the positive birthing experiences I had.

John

I'll never forget the moment Elijah was handed to me for the first time. I was sitting in the waiting room, nervously praying everything would be OK. Jade was in the operating theatre, and I was trying not to think of that iconic scene from *Alien*, where the creature bursts out of Sigourney Weaver's torso.

I waited for around thirty minutes before a nurse popped her head out and said, 'Mum and baby are both OK and we'll bring the baby out to you in a minute while Mum comes round.' A few minutes later, they passed me this little bundle of mostly towels, and somewhere amid the cotton was my sweet little prince. I filmed a video immediately for Jade, as I didn't want her to miss this moment. Within seconds of starting to film, Elijah was poking his tongue out of his mouth like a little lizard, and he was trying to suckle my fingers, the towel and anything he could turn his head to reach. He's not stopped asking for food ever since.

Once Jade had come round, we went to see her, and in a dazed state she fed Elijah for the first time. What a pro. It was such a precious moment, but it wasn't an easy road to get here.

What about the act of parenting itself? Once you've been handed the child, what next? I saw a post on Instagram that said, 'Being a parent is literally the most selfish thing you can do' – the argument being that there's nothing more self-indulgent or self-idolising than creating a mini-clone of yourself. Unsurprisingly, this argument came from somebody who, you guessed it, did not have kids.

Don't get me wrong, it isn't that there is nothing remotely selfish about having children. The motives of those who want to become parents vary greatly, and there is probably at least a modicum of self-interest permeating almost every decision we make. As many have argued, there may be no such thing as a truly altruistic act (probably other than dying for someone), but to label parenthood 'the most selfish thing someone can do' feels to me like a stretch. Particularly when it's blatantly obvious to anyone who has spent time with parents – especially the zombified guardians of tiny children – that the act of parenting children is one of the most exhausting, self-sacrificial responsibilities someone can sign themselves up for. Say goodbye to lie-ins, your figure, your privacy, your money, your tidy house, your sleep and your sanity. Say hello to tantrums, every sickness bug on the planet, premature grey hairs, worry, mum/dad-guilt and pooing with an audience.

Of course, that isn't to say I believe choosing *not* to be a parent is selfish (although the content creator mentioned above did have a list of 400 reasons why she'd chosen not to have kids, which included things like 'So I can spend all my money on myself', but that's by the by). It's certainly true that there can be selfless reasons to not have children, and there are people who for one reason or another aren't able to make that choice for themselves. But I would say that nothing has forced me to look outside of myself like cohabiting with the narcissistic, sociopathic, gaslighters we know as toddlers.

Jade

I find the 'selfish' question interesting. On the one hand, parenthood shone a light on the areas of my life where I probably was and can be quite selfish. You don't realise quite how much you do for yourself until you're suddenly unable to.

I need to confess something here. I'm going to be transparent. I find much of motherhood either very boring and uninspiring or very overwhelming and unrelenting. There, I said it. This isn't the place for tips on perfect parenting. The mum-life seems to perpetually swing back and forth between mundanity and insanity. Mums, am I alone in thinking this?

I think some of my struggle was a result of spending almost three of the first five years of motherhood on bedrest for up to twenty hours a day. John was very hands on, but he was working full time for a church, and we had no wider family around us for those first five years. To say it was tough at times would be putting it mildly.

I'm aware I'm not the only woman to struggle with pregnancy and having children, and I really hope this doesn't make you feel bad if you have also had your own personal struggle but don't have the specific physical struggle I have – pain is relative. I only say that because it's something I hear sometimes. 'Wow, and I thought my first year of parenthood was tough!' For all of us mums, motherhood often doesn't turn out the way we expect, does it? If it has for you, just know that the rest of us don't like you.

As a result, I had to rethink what it means to be a parent. One thing bedrest afforded me was a lot of thinking time. I had to deal with the anxiety of wondering how my disability would affect my son and how it would shape his childhood. Would he be bullied? Would he grow up resentful or feel he'd missed out? Was it even possible to be both paralysed and a good mum?

The harsh reality was that I couldn't avoid my shortcomings. Instead, the only positive choice I could make was to embrace them. I think that's something all mothers realise sooner or later. While my struggles are different from yours, I don't believe I'm alone. Every mother has maternal struggles. Whatever your obstacles or limitations, the external pressures on us as mums (and simply as women) can feel insurmountable at times. The pressure to have a career while raising children, to own, design and maintain the perfect home, to stay in shape, to cook the latest healthy, organic, gluten-free, vegan, Michelin-starred food for all the family – it's never ending! And those pressures have only been heightened by the juggernaut of social media.

The result can be that we conflate being busy with being productive. This in turn can cause us to get our sense of identity and self-worth from our productivity as a mother. Then we inevitably fall short and the mum guilt kicks in. This is an epidemic. So, what's the answer? How do we shrug off the pressures, raise well-rounded, content children, and remain sane ourselves?

I remember as a child my parents had the Bible verse 'Be still, and know that I am God' (Psalm 46:10) framed on our wall. I love that verse – it's brought me great comfort over the years – but being 'still' as a mum? With lively kids? Well, that isn't always possible. However, through studying theology as an adult, I discovered that the word 'still' doesn't actually mean motionless; it's more of a mentality. It's an invitation to surrender – something I've been forced to become familiar with. Surrendering to my paralysis and its limitations has been a long, tough journey, but I think that accepting my circumstances and giving them to God has helped me to learn patience and not pour pressure on myself to be someone I simply can't be.

As someone who's been very limited with what they can do and where they can go with their kids, I've learned the greatest gift I can give them is not what I can *do* for them but who I can *be* to them. I believe wholeheartedly that this is true for every mum. I want to be someone they see modelling womanhood, demonstrating healthy marriage, displaying resilience, exemplifying integrity, being dependable and living out authentic faith. These things aren't tied to my circumstances, as none of them require working legs!

I realised early on that there was a handful of things I probably wasn't going to be able to enjoy with my children. Things like walking along the beach with them or playing sports. But most of these things fell into the category of 'nice-to-haves', not 'must-haves'. When I reflected on my childhood, there weren't many things my mum did with me and my sister that I wouldn't be able to do with my kids, if and when that time came.

There isn't a single need my children have that I cannot meet. Your children don't need you to trampoline with them; they just need your love, attention, support and provision. There are many ways to give them those things. I give them my time, wisdom, energy and *presence*. No, I'll never run along the beach with the kids, but to be honest, John needs the exercise.

I may be dependent on the help of others at times, but *everyone* with children is dependent on others. That could be sharing the parental load with friends, family, child support or the school system, the list goes on. We all need help. If you can look at yourself at the end of each day and honestly say you did your best, then you should be proud of what you manage to achieve. Some days that might feel like you've smashed it; other days you may barely keep your head above water.

The heart behind the question 'Isn't it a bit selfish of you to have kids?' probably stems from one of two places: the idealistic and unattainable notions of perfection from mums or from a misunderstanding of disability and all that I'm able to do. Selfishness is when we place our self-interest above our willingness to sacrifice for others. As such, I believe the only selfish parents are the ones who choose to be absent parents. (Note the emphasis here is on *choose*. I'm aware that situations such as addiction, poverty and mental health disorders can mean that many parents who deeply love their children find themselves unable to care for them in the way they would like.) In reality, it's not having children that is selfish. It's choosing not to look after them in the way that every child deserves.

8

Q: How do you get out of bed in the morning?

A. Courtesy of my five-year-old human alarm clock and a lot of caffeine.

Jade

There's lots to get up for! Most days I don't think about my disability really. People project their feelings and fears onto me a lot. I get comments like, 'If I went through what you've been through, honestly I think I'd rather die.' First, none taken… and second, you wouldn't. In some ways, having a disability is a bit like ageing – everyone's body will fail them eventually – only I experienced difficulty walking about seventy years earlier than average. And coping with a disability that can't be healed? Once again, it's like getting older. It is what it is and it certainly beats the alternative.

John

There are many quotes that I absolutely love from the professional basketball coach and Christian John Wooden. John was the single biggest influence on the character Ted Lasso according to the show's writer and lead actor Jason Sudeikis. One of my favourites has to be: 'Things turn out best for the people who make the best of the way things turn out.'[1]

---

1   John Wooden and Jack Tobin, *They Call Me Coach* (New York: McGraw Hill, 2003).

That isn't to say we don't genuinely mourn when difficult things happen. This isn't about turning a blind eye to our pain or throwing ourselves into toxic optimism. Both of those will catch up with us sooner or later. It's about recognising that self-pity has a shelf life, and that shelf life will be different for each of us. Your resilience and the length of time you need to process pain can depend on a number of factors, like the extremity of what you've been through, your unique personality and how sensitive you are. I think all of us know that while we need time to heal, we mustn't wallow. There's a difference between being a victim and playing the victim. It can be hard not to succumb to the latter.

There's a popular theory put forward by a bloke called Gary Chapman that there are five love languages.[2] He suggests that we all relate to each of them, but we have different preferences. The five types are: words of affirmation, physical touch, quality time, acts of service and gift-giving. Some of these you will relate to more than others. When I reflect on people who are prone to playing the victim or wallowing, I wonder if they do this because they get a lot of love and attention when they're struggling. That attention can give us a huge hit of dopamine and the feeling can become almost addictive. Think about it: when you're in hospital it's horrible. When you've first had an accident or an operation it's tremendously tough and you would do anything to not feel the way you do. But when you start to recover, all the attention and love you once needed remains very attractive. Only now you can have the love without the pain. Having people visit you means you often receive love in each of the five ways we've discussed. People bring gifts and cards and grapes. You may get to spend quality time with people when usually carving out the time to see them can be tough. You get hugs and maybe a massage to aid the healing, people will cook you meals and help you out, and they may verbally express how much they love you and how worried they have been about you. Don't get me wrong – being unwell can be horrendous. But

---

2   Gary Chapman, *The Five Love Languages: The secret to love that lasts* (Chicago, IL: Moody Press, 2009).

we must be wary of falling into the trap of playing the victim. In fact, I bet your mind has already gone to someone you know who does this. Maybe it's been going on for years. Frustrating, isn't it? Possibly upsetting if that person is someone you love very much and you want to see them thrive.

That was one of the most attractive things about Jade for me. Despite all she had endured, she was one of the most healthy people I knew. Not physically, obviously – her spine was fused and her legs were in absolute tatters, but emotionally and relationally. She came across so strong, confident and at ease with herself, and that self-assurance put everyone around her at ease too.

I loved that Jade didn't seem to need others' seal of approval. She just got on with being herself and enjoying her life. She also seemed secure and happy, whether she ever found a romantic relationship or not. In fact, she was probably happier when she was single, but let's not dwell on that.

Many of us try to find our identity in the wrong places. Some people only feel they are valued, wanted and attractive if they are in a relationship. In reality, you don't need anyone else to complete you. You're not looking for your other half – you are already whole. Seeing that Jade didn't *need* me, but entered into the relationship for what she could give not get, was very attractive. She offered an emotionally stable relationship with the love and sacrifice needed to make it work in the long term. And I offered jokes.

Jade

Some people are motivated to get up each day by their dreams and goals. When those dreams are taken away from them, so is their motivation. As I was twelve when I was paralysed, I didn't have big dreams. Well, actually... I did want to be a singer and Beyoncé's backing dancer when I was nine, so let me rephrase that: I didn't have any *realistic* dreams.

Often our hopes and dreams are shaped by our experiences and upbringing. You don't have dreams of being a concert cellist if you've grown up in poverty and have never seen a cello. Everyone has limitations put on them. It's hard to have hopes and dreams until you know what you're capable of. It's one of the reasons why representation is very important. The more I see other wheelchair users doing things, the more I get to see that perhaps my horizons are bigger than I previously realised.

My dream was basically to have the most normal life possible, and I think I've come pretty close. I've got a degree, a home, gorgeous kids and I guess John's all right. Have I achieved a lot? Some might say no, but as far as I'm concerned I've hit everything on my list so far, so that's a 100% hit rate. Oh, and now a best-selling book... (Tell your friends. Seriously, though, send a friend a link to this and don't read John's next bit until you've done it. Thanks so much.)

John

One of the ongoing arguments Jade and I have is around goals and the balance between optimism and naivety, and pessimism and realism. Often, I think I'm optimistic and Jade's pessimistic. Jade thinks she's a realist and I'm a naive dreamer who talks a good game, gets carried away, runs out of steam and collapses on the sofa to play Football Manager. Ultimately, I've concluded that it's an issue of semantics and I think we're both right. Jade doesn't agree.

When I reflect on our different outlooks on life, I wonder if they are, in part, a result of our different experiences, which have led to us developing different coping mechanisms. The world has taught Jade not to get her hopes up. She has to be prepared that whenever she has a desire to do something, it might not be possible for her. As I'm an ambitious 'let's give it a shot' kind of person, this makes me want to cry. I hate that her experience is regularly one of disappointment and managing frustrations.

If I have an idea, I can enthusiastically pitch it to Jade (complete with hand gestures) and her response is never, 'Let's do this!' It's usually, 'Hmm! Have we considered everything?' I'm told by Jade that this isn't pessimism but a thing called 'processing' or 'considered thinking'.

I remember being slightly surprised by how much Jade baulked at the idea she was 'pessimistic', but on reflection I think it's similar to my frustration when she implies that I'm impatient. Growing up, I was always told how patient I was with my younger siblings. Jade has grown up being told how optimistic and positive she is, considering all she's been through. So why is it we sometimes have the opposite view of one another?

I think it's partly because in this area I'm *such* a positive dreamer that almost everyone seems pessimistic compared to me, and Jade's so supernaturally patient that, compared to her, everyone seems like one of those angry TV chefs with a double-cooked chip on their shoulder. It may also be that married life gives you a 'warts and all' view behind the curtain of each other's lives, which random friends don't see, but I think some of it is simply the result of our differing challenges. In reality, my ADHD diagnosis probably means that I do lack patience when compared to a neurotypical person. Two of the symptoms of ADHD are that you struggle when over-stimulated and can experience emotional dysregulation. This means that under the surface I am continually pushing down frustrations until I get to the point when I can no longer keep them in. For those around me, like Jade and the kids, all they see is the outburst that comes, seemingly, from nowhere. So while I feel as though I've been incredibly patient and my patience has finally been exhausted, to others it can feel as if I'm quick to anger.

Similarly, for Jade, she can come across as pessimistic compared to me when she pauses to consider what I see as incredibly exciting 'no-brainer' ideas, but that's because her world-view is one partly shaped by continual disappointments and the lack of opportunity that an inaccessible world gives her.

So we all view and assess things from our own vantage points and what we see as 'normal'.

Jade

Despite my life being pretty full and happy, there are obvious challenges and frustrations – as well as the not-so-obvious ones. Most people I speak to usually think of stairs, without realising that the bigger nemeses are kerbs and potholes. This has meant that for most of my adult life, whenever outdoors, I've been staring at the floor, checking I'm not going to hit uneven ground and be catapulted out of my chair into another leg-breaking injury. Friends have remarked that I never notice them if they see me out and about, but it's because I'm so focused on the floor. I can't enjoy my surroundings.

When I crowdfunded for my motorised all-terrain Trekinetic wheelchair and was finally able to enjoy a coffee on the go and take in my surroundings, it made John cry. Even though we'd been married for six years, he'd never fully realised how my disability impacted such simple things like enjoying a family walk.

One of the biggest banes of my existence is toilets. Not just being walked in on, à la Dubai, but the general state and availability of accessible toilets. I love to travel and explore new places, but the reality of doing this is incredibly daunting for me and for most people with a disability. The challenges start long before you even set foot on a flight. You have to notify the airline that you have a disability and require special assistance for both the airport and the flight itself. Sadly, it's not a given that notifying the airline means they will have put the necessary procedures in place for you. On the day, they will often still not be expecting you, as information seems to regularly slip through the cracks with different departments not communicating effectively. This has led to incredibly frustrating circumstances, like not being boarded onto the flight at the right time and holding up the plane's departure for thirty minutes, only to get onto the plane to face the judgemental stares of annoyed passengers who assume that I've been frolicking around in duty free. I've also been forgotten about for almost an hour following the plane's arrival at our destination, when every other passenger had disembarked long before.

The worst part of flying is probably that my wheelchair has to be taken and stowed with the cargo, so once I'm seated on the plane I have the worry that my chair won't be treated with the necessary care. We've received many comments on social media from wheelchair users saying they no longer fly abroad because of the damage baggage handlers have done to their wheelchairs in the past. I've had some minimal, cosmetic damage, like chipped paint, but also some more significant damage, like big dents in the frame, and one time they lost my chair altogether for about an hour. We eventually found it completely unattended by the baggage carousel – anyone could have taken it!

The other frustration with having my chair stowed in cargo is that I have no easy way of using the bathroom independently. Due to the narrow design of every plane I've been on, a standard wheelchair doesn't fit down the aisle, so paraplegic flyers need to use the airline 'aisle chair' – imagine something the width of a workout bench that's been bent into a seat shape and had small wheels stuck on it. If you're lucky, you might be able to fit one bum cheek on it. It's ridiculous and it's only needed because they made the aisles on planes so narrow in the first place. I can't wheel myself in it because there are no big wheels I can use to propel myself and it doesn't fit in the bathroom because airplane bathrooms are about the size of a cereal box. That's when they get the next-size-down chair, the airline's ultra slimline toilet wheelchair. I'm kidding. I'm sure they've thought of it, but so far science has been unable to design a chair small enough to fit into such a minute space.

So how do I go to the bathroom on a plane? With difficulty. On short-haul flights I tend to limit what I drink and avoid using the toilet completely, if possible. On a long-haul flight, it's helpful for John to lift me from the aisle chair and place me onto the toilet. He then closes the concertina door and waits for me, to help me back into the aisle chair. On some occasions, due to the size of the toilets, I've had to transfer without help, which is incredibly challenging and stressful. Sometimes airline staff have even told me their insurance doesn't cover anyone else assisting me, so only they can assist me, but often they're not trained or aware of my needs. This whole ordeal is highly indiscreet. I can feel very self-conscious with so many eyes watching me as if I'm in an in-flight entertainment documentary.

When I tell people this, they're often shocked, but to date I have never been on a plane, or flown with an airline, that has a disabled toilet onboard. Occasionally, I've heard people make the point that the limited space means it's impossible to include a disabled loo, but given that planes have space for full beds and showers for first class passengers, logistics and space aren't the issue; money-pinching greed is. Airlines could easily remove a row of seats and extend one toilet on every plane, but unless they are put under pressure to change and it's made illegal not to accommodate those with disabilities, they won't. But it should be illegal. If you are capable of independently using the toilet at home, in public and even on trains, why should planes be any different? It's ableism and just one example where companies are allowed to put profits over people. Ironically, this penny-pinching is probably counting against airlines in the long run, as they would likely make more money if they included such facilities. The addition of wider bathrooms would be welcomed by more than just the disabled community, as mothers of small children also know the impossible task of changing a nappy in such a tight space.

Even the companies that do make the effort to be inclusive are often more concerned about box-ticking than well-considered adaptations. There's a fancy hotel in Dubai – one of the most exclusive hotels in the world – which holds an annual music festival on the beach, and it happened to fall during our engagement holiday. However, when we called to enquire about accessibility, we were told they didn't have an accessible Portaloo. When we asked what we were supposed to do, they told us that the hotel would be happy to pay for a chauffeur-driven car to take me to the nearest accessible toilet, over a mile away, whenever I needed the bathroom. While I applauded them for their willingness to go the extra mile, given the weather in Dubai and the need to hydrate, it would probably have meant me missing a lot of the evening. Unsurprisingly, we didn't go.

On another occasion, John and I went to a twelve-course tasting-menu dinner in London while we were dating. About halfway through the evening I went to find the disabled toilet and as I opened the door with my radar key, I discovered it was full of stock! Obviously outraged I complained and they apologised, before saying, 'We just don't get many disabled people come here.'

'Of course you don't!' I replied. 'They come once and never come back, because you've turned our toilet into a stockroom!'

The worst was when a restaurant had converted their disabled bathroom into a manager's office. There was even a desk and swivel chair. I wish I was joking.

Companies that boast 'everyone is welcome here' but don't have disabled facilities should take that sign down. If everyone is welcome, but only so long as those without toilets are happy to dehydrate or wet themselves, then not everyone is welcome. How can you feel welcome when your basic needs are not met?

John

Hearing these stories, and being by her side for many of them, does help me to understand why it can be hard for Jade to be optimistic at times. Outside of accessibility, though, she's hopeful for each day and she's infinitely better than I am at living in the moment. This does mean she's not always as forward-thinking as I am, but it doesn't hold her back. Despite the way the world treats her, she resiliently pushes through and refuses to let life get her down. I guess we balance each other out well. We wouldn't have this book if it wasn't for the wisdom Jade has gained through her story, but we wouldn't have written it if it wasn't for my motivation to aim high.

Jade

I think many people believe the worst thing that could happen to a person has happened to me. Short of death or an even more severe disability, my life is many people's worst nightmare, and, as I've already mentioned, I've had people tell me that if they were in my position they probably wouldn't want to live. Since becoming paralysed, one of my favourite Bible verses is Proverbs 18:14: 'The human spirit can endure in sickness, but a crushed spirit who can bear?' I love it because it doesn't shy away from the hardships of sickness. It uses the word 'endure' and it *is* an endurance being disabled or having a chronic illness. There are times when it can feel unbearable. But there is something far worse than that – having a crushed spirit. Being without hope takes more away from a person's life than any physical illness can.

I think many of us have experienced moments in our lives when we've felt crushed or oppressed or overwhelmed, and I love how God doesn't shy away from that. He knows exactly what we're going through and he knows the struggles we have, but we're not in it alone and that makes such a difference. To me, God isn't this far-removed being, up in the sky; he's in the suffering with us. Jesus himself was well acquainted with suffering, so he knows how it feels to be crushed by life, rejected by friends, overwhelmed with stress, to have the walls of life close in on you and to have to endure excruciating physical pain. So when we call out to God in our pain and suffering, we aren't reaching out to a God who doesn't have first-hand experiences like ours. We can never say to Jesus, 'It's easy for you! You don't know what it's like!'

I have an everlasting joy and hope that isn't based on some kind of arbitrary optimism that one day things will turn out OK. My hope is based on Jesus – the one who endured pain so that one day we won't have to. My experience is that he draws near to us in those hard times, because I wouldn't have survived it without him. He's the only one who can stop us from being crushed. He's the biggest reason I can embrace each day with joy and hope.

9

Q: Do any disabled jokes offend you?

A. Yes, but only the lame ones.

Jade

When it comes to humour, I'm pretty unoffendable. If a joke is funny, or even if it's not but I can tell it doesn't come from a bad place, I don't mind. It's incredibly rare that I take jokes to heart or get upset by them. I think this is partly because, in my experience, when people make disabled jokes they're just testing the waters. They're trying to work out where the line is when it comes to cheeky comments.

That said, my advice to those who ask me about dark humour is always to follow the lead of the person themselves. I'm comfortable with jokes and recognise it's mostly a bid to connect with me. It's rarely a person's attempt to point-score or put me down or elevate themselves above me. If I'm being completely candid, I think a lot of people already feel they're slightly above me anyway. By that, I don't mean most people arrogantly view themselves as better than me, that would be particularly mean-spirited. But I do pick up on a subconscious, pitying approach. People can demonstrate a sense of sympathy towards me and that can sometimes manifest itself in a patronising way. I think in some ways it's understandable. The general feeling among able-bodied people is that, if possible, they would very much like to not become paralysed. I share that view. It's not ideal, what happened to me.

That said, the disability doesn't make me sub-human, unworthy of love or any less valuable. Along with every person on the planet, I deserve dignity and respect. That feeling of having to defend my position is one of the reasons I love humour so much. It can be a leveller. As far as I'm concerned, it's a British rite of passage to mock your mates. I'm sure other cultures do the same, but I know that not all of them do. In the UK, to tease someone doesn't mean you don't like them. If anything, it probably means you do. Because of that, I tend to give people the benefit of the doubt.

I do, however, have some advice to save you causing offence if you're toying with the idea of unleashing some dark humour and irony. First, ask yourself: 'How well do I know this person?' This also applies to asking intrusive questions and offering well-intentioned but poorly delivered encouragement. The classic joke I get from strangers is, 'Wow, you're good at that, aren't you? Do you have a driver's licence for that thing?' As if I'm a toddler on a scooter! My polite response is, 'Well, I've had plenty of practice!' but my inner voice is saying, 'Who would have thought, eh? Being forced to use something every single day, any time I want to get anywhere, for *twenty years* because I was left cruelly disabled as a teenager, would result in me being proficient at, let's be honest, the pretty basic skill of wheeling myself around?! You don't hear me saying, "Wow, you're good with those legs, aren't you?"!'

I'm aware that might seem a bit over the top when you consider that the people who say these things don't know I use a wheelchair full-time and they don't know how long I've been disabled. But that's sort of the point: they don't know me at all, so it would be better to tread carefully (pun intended).

When it comes to close family and friends, it's totally different. They will relentlessly take the mick out of me, but that's within the context of a safe relationship. I know there's no truth in what they're saying. I'm not worried that they might *genuinely* have a low view of disabled people. I know they love me.

A few years ago, I went into a Starbucks with my friend. Coincidentally, my mum was also there, already in the queue with her friend. At one point she turned around, saw me, then turned back to her friend and said, 'Can you believe it?! They're letting disabled people in here now!' On reflection, she was probably speaking a little too loud, as those standing near her in the queue looked visibly shocked and appalled. I think mum was expecting me just to laugh it off and come over to her so everyone would know she wasn't actually a terrible person. But I saw my moment. I knew that to amp up the funny I should pretend I didn't know her. So I just sat there, looking pathetic and hurt. I even added a quiet and awkward 'Did you hear what that lady just said?' to my friend. When I say that it was funnier, I do of course mean funnier for me. It wasn't funnier for everyone else, and it definitely wasn't funnier for Mum. But to be fair she did start it. If she's going to show off to her friends, I'm going to show off to mine.

That story has become a great one to tell at dinner. Of course I wasn't actually hurt. We obviously had such a close pre-existing relationship that my mum knew the line and understood my humour. That isn't to say humour can't be used as a way of breaking the ice with somebody, but again it's better to let the disabled person start that process. When you are the minority in a social setting for any reason, it can sometimes feel hard to integrate yourself into the group. As a result, disabled people will often choose to remove the potential awkwardness by being self-deprecating. But when someone in the majority, able-bodied group chooses to point out the one thing that makes you different from everyone else, it's likely to cause upset.

John

In March 2023, when I found out I had ADHD, it was an eye-opening discovery that explained so many of the frustrations and limitations I had experienced. Part of having ADHD means you can be impulsive, you overshare and say things without thinking. This can obviously have its downsides. I can also be over-familiar with people – although I'm not sure if that comes with the diagnosis or it's just what I'm like. I hope it's part of my charm as I seem to get away with it 99% of the time.

Do any disabled jokes offend you?

I remember the first joke I made about Jade's disability. It was when we had just met at uni. I can't remember what led us to this point, but Jade made a joke about my short stature. Before I had chance to think about it, I shot back, 'Well, at least I'm taller than you,' and then used my hand to measure her height, signalling that she came up to my midriff from her sitting position. Thankfully she laughed and it was taken as playful banter. Looking back, I think that's because she started the teasing and I was just sparring with her. Physical jab for physical jab. Seeing her as a worthy opponent, rather than patronisingly seeing her as someone I couldn't fire back with.

But a joke landing well isn't always a given, is it? Sometimes we say something that sounds funny in our head, but by the time it leaves our mouth we realise maybe we should have kept it to ourselves. What if she had been offended? And if she had, would that have made it offensive? Does it depend on the intentions of the person saying it? Or are some things simply unsayable, even if the heart behind those things is good? It's a tough road to navigate.

Art is subjective, and given that there is an art to humour, it can be incredibly difficult to make hard-and-fast rules. In fact, part of the beauty of the uniqueness of every individual is that we *don't* all find the same things funny. As Jimmy Carr once said: 'If you think I'm funny, you're right. If you think I'm not funny, you're right.'[1]

Does that mean, then, we can just shrug and say, 'Each to their own'? Well, no. We all have lines that we don't want to be crossed, and part of loving others and living in harmony with them is learning empathy for those who struggle in ways we don't. That doesn't mean we must feel guilty for offending someone every time it happens – we all know people who are very quick to take offence. However, we shouldn't assume that just because we don't find something offensive we have licence to recklessly upset those who have a different threshold.

I realise this may all be rather deep, but I think it's important. The humour Jade and I share online may be a little dark for some

---

1 J. Carr, 'The Legend of Rack's Mum', X, 12 January 2023: https://twitter.com/jimmycarr/status/1613566473821163520 (accessed 27 March 2024).

tastes. For some, jokingly calling Jade lazy or boring for not wanting to try things that her disability makes difficult or impossible is the height of insensitivity. I've been accused a couple of times of hating wheelchair users.

Interestingly, that's only ever been an accusation levelled at me by people who are not paralysed. To my knowledge, I've never had a comment along those lines from someone with a disability. I think we can attribute some of this to virtue signalling, which frankly is the height of narcissism. It's not actually helping the situation, it's entirely about keeping up appearances, and guess what? No one is keeping score. No one is thinking, 'Well, I know Sarah's a good person, because six months ago she said that she found a disabled joke on TikTok offensive.'

When it comes to cracking jokes, we live in interesting times. People can lose their whole career over a joke, so the stakes are pretty high. Should that be a reality? Well, and get used to hearing this, it depends. What was the joke? What was the intention of the joke? Why do people find it offensive? Why was it funny? In what context was it shared? Was the person remorseful? What or who was the target? All of these only beg further, bigger questions. Who polices comedy? Should we police comedy? What are the dangers if we police it too forcefully? What are the dangers if we police it too leniently?

All these questions and more have been incredibly fascinating to me for most of my life. I love to joke – you may be aware? – it's probably my favourite thing. Not only does it bring joy to people, but it *connects* me with people too. Danish comedian and pianist Victor Borge is often quoted as saying, 'Laughter is the shortest distance between two people,' and it's been bridging gaps between me and those around me since I can remember.

So why is it that a device that can be so powerful in helping us connect with others can also go so badly wrong? Because it's a tool, and every tool can be used well or misused. A scalpel can save someone's life in the right hands of a surgeon, or end someone's life in the wrong hands of a psychopath. In every interaction we have, humorous or otherwise, things go wrong when one party no longer feels safe. Imagine a scenario where you're jokingly mocked about a genuine insecurity you have. The mocker is a good friend who you believe loves you, but they're not so close to you that they are aware you are insecure about the thing they just mocked. How do you react? I'll wager it will depend on how safe you feel. Perhaps, because you trust your friend loves you and you know they are unaware of your insecurity, you'll laugh it off. But switch the context of the scenario to an ex-partner who knows how insecure you are about the very thing they've just mocked, and *doesn't* love you, and things feel very different, don't they? Suddenly the same joke is offensive and hurtful. Context is crucial and the perceived safety of each party is paramount for healthy and fun interactions.

So how do we navigate offence, both when we take it and when others take it in response to something we've said? In the book *Crucial Conversations: Tools for talking when stakes are high*,[2] the authors Patterson, Grenny, McMillan and Switzler sought to understand why some people were so popular, effective and influential in the workplace. They concluded the number one reason was that they were fantastic at navigating high-stakes conversations. They explained that, in difficult conversations, there's an influencing factor that falls somewhere in between the words said and how we feel about them. They call it 'the story we tell ourselves'. One of the fatal traps each of us can fall into is assuming we know the full story. We think we understand the context and make assumptions. Maybe we assume the person was being cruel and perhaps needs educating. We like to think we have all the facts. But it's never that simple.

This applies not only to high-stakes conversations but also to humour. So if we go back to the friend who mocked our insecurity, the story we may tell ourselves is, 'They were just playing and they weren't to know.' But the other story we may tell ourselves, if we're not feeling so generous that day, is, 'Why would they tease me about something like that? Why would they so carelessly hurt me

---

2   K. Patterson, J. Grenny, R. McMillan and A. Switzler, *Crucial Conversations: Tools for talking when stakes are high* (McGraw Hill Contemporary, 2002).

for no reason?' When we feel unsafe or threatened we go into fight or flight mode, so we're likely to either fire a barbed comment back or withdraw into ourselves. This is rarely beneficial in relationships. Often people are quick to jump to conclusions based on their own experiences, but we would live happier, more enjoyable, lives if we opted to give people the benefit of the doubt.

To give a real-life example, one video we shared was of our daughter running over to me and Jade in the park, loudly declaring, 'Daddy, there's a lady in a wheelchair like Mummy!' I then say, 'Was there? That's cool. Was it a good wheelchair?' Our daughter, the sassy three-year-old that she is, then totally u-turns on me, and goes from excited to savage in the blink of an eye. 'NO!' she declares. I then laugh really hard.

To say this video was divisive would be an understatement. We got thousands of comments. Some were as simple as, 'Oh my gosh! I love her. She's so funny! Kids, eh?!' But others took a different approach: 'This is disgusting. Not everyone can afford a nice wheelchair! Just because you guys were born with silver spoons in your mouths, why would you think it's OK to laugh at people less fortunate?'; 'Why did the dad ask if the wheelchair was good? SO snobby and only encourages his daughter to be judgemental in the future!'; 'Why did the dad laugh at the poor woman with the bad wheelchair? Disgusting!'; 'I hope to see a full apology to this poor person. You should be befriending such people and raising money for them using your platform.' And finally, and totally unrelated, 'Why does that little girl have two black eyes and horrendous sunburn? What negligent parents!' (This was simply an exposure issue with the video, so if I was neglecting anything it was good lighting.)

You see the problem when we assume to know the full story? One person shared how triggering this was for them because they were mercilessly teased for having a bad wheelchair growing up, and they'd leapt to the conclusion that we were doing the same. Often, our personal circumstances skew our perspective. This can leave us feeling triggered and hurt. As painful as that may be, it doesn't mean the joke-teller or story-sharer has actually done anything wrong. The cross-over in subject matter doesn't mean there is any intention of mean-spirited bullying.

What's particularly interesting is that you don't actually see the other wheelchair user mentioned in the video at all. All we know is she is a lady in a wheelchair. So it was surprising how many people took a three-year-old's sassy wheelchair assessment as gospel, and then labelled it bullying. The other woman was actually in a very nice, motorised wheelchair, very similar to Jade's. I would also add that a child has absolutely no idea what constitutes a 'good' wheelchair anyway.

Ricky Gervais once said that 'offense is taken, not given',[3] and while that may be a little simplistic, I think there's some truth to it. In reality, we rarely have all the facts. So in the instances when we're quicker to get offended than we are to seek to understand, I think Ricky is bang on the money. When I hear that someone is offended by a statement that is pretty ambiguous, what I actually hear is: 'I choose to believe the worst about people.'

Here's another ridiculous example. I used the word 'savage' in a video and was told in the comments that I was a disgrace and should be cancelled for using a term so deeply offensive to indigenous people. This sounds serious, right? Until you realise that I was calling my daughter savage for roasting me with one of her sassy comments. I asked how I could be abusing the Native American people when I was talking about my Caucasian child and the word just means 'brutal' in this context. The response I got was, 'The context is irrelevant. The term is offensive.' To which I replied, 'I hope you never refer to the healthy plants in the grocery stores as "vegetables", then, because that term has been used as a derogatory term for people in wheelchairs.' Just when you'd think the exchange couldn't get more ridiculous, the person doubled down, accepted that I had made a good point, conceded they probably shouldn't be referring to vegetables as vegetables and promised to think about how they could use healthier, more

3   R. Gervais, X, 15 November 2012: https://twitter.com/rickygervais/status/269026306203738113 (accessed 27 March 2024).

inclusive, language in future. I wish I was joking. If you're a persecuted parsnip reading this, or an oppressed onion, you'll be pleased to hear that liberation is coming. The days of being likened to disabled people will be a thing of the past.

Another concern is the breadth of authority we feel we can have when speaking on behalf of others – even sometimes when we speak for others from within our 'people group'. When people leave comments on our videos like, 'That is offensive to wheelchair users,' I always think, 'That's weird, because the joke was actually my wife's idea. So clearly not *all* wheelchair users find it offensive.'

At one point, one of my videos went viral and reached a part of Asia. When I woke up, I had a load of comments posted between 3 and 4 a.m., saying things like, 'You shouldn't call your wife disabled! The correct term is "differently abled".' Except I already knew it wasn't. Not for Jade. When I told Jade that people on the internet were saying I had to refer to her as differently abled now, she mock-retched in her mouth and told me she'd leave me if I did. She *hates* that term. So we need to be careful not to think we can speak with authority for anyone other than, well, ourselves.

Jade

Gosh, John's got a bit serious here, hasn't he? Need another funny story? Don't worry, I've got a couple for you. Disclaimer: these will both act as examples of another serious point – is it OK for an able-bodied person to use a disabled person's mobility aid? You'll still laugh, but I'm afraid school's not out just yet.

I went into hospital to have surgery while I was at university. My friend Luke came to visit me, but there was no chair in my room, so as I lay in my hospital bed recovering from my op, Luke sat in my vacant wheelchair, chatting with me. I was then told I needed to go for an X-ray and I said to Luke that he may as well come down with me. Luke said, 'Is it OK if I just come down in your wheelchair?' as he'd never used one and was sitting in it anyway. I laughed and said, 'Sure, why not!' Modes of transport confirmed, when the porters arrived to take me down to the X-ray department, Luke followed us in my chair.

The first awkward moment came when we got to the lift and couldn't fit my big hospital bed plus the wheelchair in. So I had to go down to the right floor and then wait while Luke hung back for the next lift and then re-joined us. He then stuck around in the waiting room while I had the X-ray. When I was done, we waited for the porters to return. But only one of them came back. We waited. Ten minutes became twenty. Twenty became thirty. The porter kept radioing his colleagues, but nobody came.

After we'd been waiting for an hour, I asked Luke to grab me a drink. Realising he wouldn't be able to hold the cup of tea and wheel himself in my chair, he jumped up and started walking to the hot drinks machine. The porter looked shocked and exclaimed, 'You can walk?!' Neither of us had properly considered that other people would assume he needed the chair. Luke replied, 'Yeah, I just wanted to take it for a spin!' The porter sighed and said, 'If I'd known you could walk, you could have helped me take her back to her room an hour ago!' Luke sheepishly apologised and then quickly ran my wheelchair back to my room before returning to help take me to my ward, where we both died of embarrassment.

Years later, John and I went to the cinema. Sometimes I stay in my chair as some screens have a gap for wheelchairs, but it's often comfier to get into the cinema seats themselves – especially in the more modern cinemas. On this occasion, I transferred from my chair into one of the seats and John tucked it away at the back of the room. As the trailers started, I noticed someone else come down the aisle in a wheelchair. This boy was fifteen or sixteen and had a huge smile on his face. I always notice other wheelchair users and I love it when I see them really enjoying life. Remarkably, he seemed to have a very similar chair to mine – the same brand, similar size, even the same scrapes on one of the wheel grips. Hang on... It was then that I realised it wasn't a similar wheelchair, it was *my* wheelchair. I leant over to John and whispered, 'That boy's in my wheelchair.' He got straight up and told the boy that he shouldn't be using my chair. Even in the dark, the lad looked visibly shocked. John returned the wheelchair to its position at the back and sat down again. Apparently, the boy thought he was playing with 'the cinema's wheelchair'.

This all begs the question of whether it's offensive to use a wheelchair when you don't need one. Well, it depends. One topic that has come up a lot in the press recently is straight from Hollywood: is it OK for an able-bodied person to play a disabled person?

It may not surprise you to hear that I have some thoughts on this one. While it is true that it's called acting for a reason, and a fundamental part of the job is pretending to be someone you are not, there is something important to note here. Sometimes I hear false equivalences bandied around on the topic of taking roles away from certain people groups. There is nothing unfair about, say, a straight actor playing a gay character, simply because it's possible for the opposite to also happen. A gay actor is perfectly capable of playing a straight character too. There are no physical limitations as a result of your sexuality. However, with many disabilities, disabled actors can't play non-disabled characters. I wouldn't be upset if a movie of my life was ever made and a lesbian actor played me. However, I would probably be sad if I was played by someone who could walk. Disabled actors already have far fewer opportunities, simply because a disabled woman cannot choose to play someone who can walk. The exception to this is when somebody needs to play both the non-disabled and then disabled version of the same character – for example, Eddie Redmayne as Professor Stephen Hawking in *The Theory of Everything*.

Back to the topic of using someone's wheelchair when you can walk. Sure you can, if you have permission from the disabled person and assuming they aren't in it at the time. I don't find it any more offensive than someone asking to borrow someone's glasses. If anything, I think those who wear glasses probably get worse comments. I've seen people try on a friend's specs and then remark, 'Wow! This is so weird. I can't see a thing. How blind are *you*!' To date, I've never had anyone sit in my wheelchair and go, 'Wow! This is so weird. You can't walk at all, can you!'

John

When many of us strive to live moral lives, why is it that we still laugh at 'offensive' jokes? I think often it can be because of shock. This laughter doesn't mean we agree with the morality of the joke; sometimes we're just surprised someone made it.

We've probably all said something outrageous to a close friend or family member – just to make them laugh. Our heart isn't full of hatred towards the person who is the butt of the joke; we don't really even believe what we're saying. In fact, we're probably saying it *precisely* because we don't believe it at all. We probably know it's wrong, but the close relational environment keeps these jokes safe. We know that's all it is – joking.

Sometimes the laughter is a release of tension. I once heard someone begin their set at a stand-up comedy night by saying, 'I hate blacks!' You could hear a pin drop; people were understandably very, *very* tense. The comedian continued, 'Which is why I buy all my camping equipment from Millets.' Huge laugh. (For those not in the UK, we have an outdoor clothing and camping store called Blacks.)

While there's a difference between saying something to a friend and a stand-up comedian cracking jokes on stage, I think there is a cross-over here. It's probably why many people like controversial comedians. While we don't know our favourite celebrities person-ally at all, it often *feels* as if we do. As such, a comedian making dark jokes, if done well, can feel like that outrageous close friend who's always treading dangerously close to the line. However, the ques-tion of motives still looms large. What if the comedian is hiding behind the idea that they're 'just jokes' but actually *does* hate the people group he's joking about? Or what if he's genuinely being ironic, but a considerable number of the audience are taking it at face value and laughing from a place of malice?

On the one hand, we've definitely become too sensitive about some things. But on the other, we can understand why those who have been through traumatic experiences might feel triggered when jokes hit on that painful subject. Yet even that doesn't automatically make the joke-teller some sort of monster. How about the person whose family died in a car crash, swerving to avoid a chicken crossing the road? Does that render any teller of the classic 'why did the chicken cross the road?' joke an offensive comedian? Of course not.

We now find ourselves in the difficult position where the exact same joke can be both offensive and inoffensive. This is why I think we need to be less conscious of what the joke itself says and more conscious of the context in which it is told. For instance, I, the husband of a disabled woman, can call my wife lazy with a cheeky wink as I happily grab her something she can't reach and she'll smile back. This is very different from a group of politicians at a meeting aiming to slash the budget for disability benefits joking and raucously laughing as they brand disabled people as lazy. Is the joke offensive or not? In short: it depends on the context.

Sadly, many of us have been manipulated by the media, who realise that the grey areas of life don't sell papers, so these days everything is either amazing or disgusting. This sensationalism is contagious, and balanced views are increasingly rare. There's a misconception that balance is unprincipled, uneducated or cowardly. Of course, playing the diplomatic card and claiming you can see all sides might be uneducated or cowardly, but being outspoken on the populist view could be too.

Jade

Some of the funniest moments I've experienced have been unintentional jokes. The effect is maximised when the joke-teller is left mortified at their unfortunate choice of words.

I was speaking at a church youth group event when one of the group leaders introduced me by saying: 'We're thrilled to have Jade Greasley [maiden name] come and speak with us tonight. Jade's got an incredible life story and I'm really excited to hear from her as she shares all about her walk with Jesus.' The woman instantly realised what she'd said. Her face fell. The room went silent. And then John and I burst out laughing and everyone joined in. It was hilarious. Everything about it was perfect: the upbeat and enthusiastic church intro, the totally unintentional Christian idiom and the mortified look on her face. Comedic perfection.

Given the number of expressions that involve bodily functions (standing, seeing, hearing, etc.), this is a frequent occurrence for those with physical disabilities. My friend Laura, a nurse, was helping a frustrated newly disabled double amputee to the toilet, when she said: 'You're doing great, don't worry. We'll have you back on your feet in no time!' Mortifying. But totally innocent.

I'm more offended by the lack of accessibility in society and the lack of opportunity for disabled people than I am by a few spicy jokes. That being said, there are terms I don't really like – 'vegetable' or 'cripple', for example. These feel dehumanising and degrading, and are rarely used in an inclusive 'I see you as a human being and this is just banter reflective of that' kind of way. Rather than including the person, these labels undermine them. I don't have much time for that.

One of the biggest struggles I have is hearing the same jokes over and over again. By that I mean the same jokes from the same people. I had a teacher at school who, upon seeing me, would always exclaim, 'Oh, here she comes – Speedy Gonzales!' It's not that the joke was offensive – just boring and outdated (I had to Google Speedy Gonzales). There's only so many times you can muster the energy for a fake laugh. Oh, and if I hear somebody make a 'really'/'wheely' pun one more time I'm going to run them over. (In my wheelchair, I mean – not my car. I'm not a psychopath.)

Having said all this, I would still prefer that we manage the risks of humour than do away with it all together. When a topic is off limits to jokes, it holds too much power. That doesn't mean you can say anything you like, but I think you can make a morally acceptable joke about *any* topic; it just depends what that joke is, how it's told and in what context. Laughter can be healing. Not physically, but emotionally and relationally.

Stealing from the thief

I love the line from Shakespeare's *Othello*: 'The robb'd that smiles steals something from the thief.'[4] In other words, when you rise above those who try to take your joy, you're the one who wins. If there are dark forces in this world actively fighting against God's vision for goodness and wholeness, it's a rebellious act of defiance to laugh. Especially, in the middle of our pain, to choose joy despite the suffering.

I know, for some, talking about God as the answer might seem odd or unnecessary. 'I love you guys, but keep your faith to yourself!' you may be thinking. And I hear that. I've tried hard to make sure that my advice is helpful to everyone, whether they face disability or any other challenge, but also whether they have faith, passionately believe there is no God or are somewhere in the middle. The thing is, it is impossible for me to talk about my life and why I'm hopeful and positive (on the whole) without talking about the reason I have that hope.

For me, it's because I believe that every single person is created in the image of God that I place high worth and value on individuals and want them to be treated with respect and dignity, no matter their ability. I remain positive because I believe that God has a plan for my life that is much bigger than my disability. I have hope because I believe that one day all pain, sadness and sickness will be a thing of the past.

There's a great series of videos called *The Bible Course*.[5] Stay with me here, I know it doesn't sound riveting, but I promise it's very engaging and they give a great analogy. They say that the hope Christians have is similar to watching a football match live versus watching it on *Match of the Day*. If you're watching a game live and the team you support is losing 2:0 in real time, that's heartbreaking for football fans. However, if they come back to win that game 3:2, there's a lot of joy in the end. Not only that, but when you watch the

---

4   W. Shakespeare, *Othello* (c.1603), Act I, scene 3, line 208.

5   https://www.biblesociety.org.uk/explore-the-bible/the-bible-course/ (accessed 12 March 2024).

highlights of the match later on that evening, you're not remotely stressed when the opposition go 1:0 and then 2:0 up. Why? Because you know the final score. You know those momentary trials are overcome in the end. You know that pain is part of the story but it isn't the end of the story. So too for us, when we have a hope that transcends our current circumstances.

This is why I love the Proverbs 18:14 Bible verse I mentioned earlier. It shows us the power of our mind, the power of hope and the power of believing in something bigger than ourselves.

10

Q: If you're a Christian, why did God let this happen? And why hasn't he healed you?

A. He never promises bad things won't happen to us or that all will be healed.

Jade

Once people know *what* happened to me their next question is: 'Why would this happen to you?' In essence, I think they're asking the age-old question, 'Why do bad things happen to good people?' Which I guess is a compliment. Whatever people think of me, it's at least reassuring to know that they don't think I'm deserving of paralysis.

I understand why people grapple with the question. In essence, they are trying to reconcile a God who is all-knowing, all-powerful and all-loving with one who would also allow such a tragedy. Especially to a card-carrying member of the Jesus club. I mean, come on, are there not members' privileges? What's particularly interesting is that this question is asked by believers and non-believers alike. If you're picturing a smug atheist unsympathetically mocking the faith of a paraplegic, you'd be wrong. Christians want to know too.

Whenever I'm asked, 'Why would God let this happen to you?' my answer is always the same: 'Why *wouldn't* this happen to me?' What makes me any different from anyone else that I should be excluded from this? Not in the pessimistic 'these things always happen to poor little me' sense, but simply because I already know that being a Christian doesn't make you immune to life's struggles. A cursory glance at the Bible is all you need, to realise some pretty bad things happen to people – and not just God's enemies, but his people too. It's one of the many things I love about the Bible: it doesn't sugar-coat the realities of life.

One of my favourite stories Jesus told is recorded in Matthew 7:24–27 and it's helped me shape how I think about suffering. He spoke about a wise builder and a foolish builder – the wise one built his house on a firm foundation, but the fool built on the sand. You don't need a theology degree to work out where this is going. When the storms came and hit the houses, the one built on secure foundations was the one that stood firm.

The primary point is that when you build your whole life on the good but temporary things of this world, what will you do when the storms come? If your whole life is your family, what happens if they are taken from you? If your whole life is your career, what do you do if you're made redundant? If your whole life is your health, what happens if you're diagnosed with a chronic health condition? Are you still you when you lose something precious? Or have you defined yourself by things that were never meant to define you? Because, as important as it may be, you're not your job. As utterly loved as they may be, you're not even your relationship to your family. And as important as walking was to me, I am not my legs. I am more than my physical health.

Yet one of the most important truths from that story is Jesus' openness about the tough things in life. Notice the storms hit *both* houses. Whether your life is built on God (who I believe is unchanging and can never be taken from you) or your life is built on something that could be here today and gone tomorrow, the storms *will* hit you. Cheery, isn't it?! Maybe not, but it's true. It's real life and we can all attest to that.

Jesus even says in John 16:33, 'In this world you will have trouble.' Not *might*, but *will*. Jesus never promised me an easy life and, let's be honest, he didn't exactly have one himself, did he? So if God's Son wasn't immune to suffering, why would we think we should be?

The beauty of what Jesus goes on to say in that verse is incredible, though: 'In this world you will have trouble. But take heart! I have overcome the world.' Jesus doesn't promise to prevent or heal all pain in this life, but he does promise there will come a day when all pain will be gone. Every tear wiped away. The happy ending every single one of us yearns for, perhaps even intuitively believes in, is I think written into our hearts by God, who promised that one day he would make all things new (Revelation 21:5).

John

I love Jade's perspective on the problem of pain. Despite living with her every day, I still regularly have my eyes opened by her wisdom and knowledge. I think many of us have found ourselves frustrated with God because we have expectations of him that he never actually promised in the first place.

As we write this, we're sitting in our favourite café in Preston. It's attached to a local church and run by many of the church members. We know the waiter, a guy called Benny, and he's just told us the most amazing news. His sister-in-law, like Jade, had transverse myelitis. It didn't leave her paralysed, but she still needed a stick to walk and, on many days, used a wheelchair due to the pain. She had only managed very wobbly steps over the last thirteen years, but he told us with amazement on his face that, having been prayed for, she'd been totally healed! He laughed with joy as he said, 'She's walking, jumping and running now. And the sensation and feeling that she had lost has been totally restored.'

He explained that he'd been hesitant to tell us, fearing that it might be bitter-sweet given Jade's current lack of healing, but we told him that's not at all how we feel and we're over the moon for her.

Jade

As Benny left, John and I chatted some more about it and how incredible the news was. And then I confessed to John, 'This feels controversial... but I'm not actually *desperate* to be healed.' He told me he got it, and I loved how well he knew me in that moment and totally understood what I meant. Don't get me wrong, being healed would be amazing. And there's a ton of things I'd love to do if I was. But I have a good life. So any big goal I've had in life I've either been able to achieve or there is no reason I won't be able to in the future.

Sometimes I think we have a one-dimensional view of what a miracle really is. Whenever we're going through trauma or suffering and we pray for healing, it's important to remember that just because God doesn't always answer in the way we hope, it doesn't mean he hasn't answered. He's not a genie in a bottle who gives us three wishes. If he's real and he's the creator of the Universe, then he's my Master, not the other way around.

John

While Jade has yet to be healed of her physical struggles, she has been healed inwardly of the emotional pain. As referenced above, Jesus saying, 'In this world you will have trouble' is actually comforting rather than threatening. I imagine it being said in an honest yet gentle tone. It's him demonstrating he knows us and all we'll have to face.

The Christian goal isn't to avoid suffering; it's to find God in the middle of it. If Jesus himself wasn't immune to suffering, it's only going to make our lives even harder if we think we're able to avoid it. Instead, it's better to take time to heal and then reflect on what you've learned through the pain, especially the things you wouldn't have learned without it, and how that has strengthened your character.

I think many of us tend to think of life as binary, classifying moments as either 'good' or 'bad'. However, it's rarely as black and white as that. Even the happiest moments aren't perfect and the lowest can have slithers of beauty. Things that might feel one way in the short-term can look very different with some distance. The gym can be painful in the moment, and even for a few days afterwards, but we know the momentary suffering of exercise is good for us in the long run. In fact, if we stopped exercising the moment a particular muscle group got tired, we would never get any stronger. There is purpose in the pain.

The Bible's book of Romans explains this with a kind of flow diagram in chapter 5, verses 3–5: 'Suffering produces perseverance; perseverance, character; and character, hope. And hope does not put us to shame, because God's love has been poured out into our hearts.' In other words, as we suffer we grow in perseverance, as we grow in perseverance we grow in character, as we grow in character and maturity we grow in hope, and when we hope in God, we will not be put to shame.

This may be one of the reasons why those who have never had to suffer for anything are the least likely to have a faith. The more privileged you are, the more you believe the lie that you can be self-sufficient, and the more self-sufficient you believe yourself to be, the less you need others – God included.

Jade

One of the worst things I've found about having a chronic illness and suffering from it is the barriers it puts up between you and everyone else. The times when my health has left me very isolated from others have been the toughest. Not simply because of the FOMO, but because of the loneliness. We don't just enjoy relational contact, we *need* it.

In Matthew 9:20–22, we read the account of Jesus healing a bleeding woman. She's been haemorrhaging for twelve years, but has the faith to know that if she can just touch Jesus' cloak, she will be healed. She reaches out and touches it and is instantly healed. What makes this even more beautiful is Jesus' response when he feels the power leave him. He says, 'Take heart, daughter... your faith has healed you.' It's easy for us to recognise the incredible impact the physical healing must have had on her life, but what we may miss, reading this through with twenty-first-century eyes, is the power of hearing herself being called 'daughter'. This healed her social identity too. Due to the Jewish cleanliness rules (spiritual cleanliness, not physical), when a woman was bleeding she was considered 'unclean' and she wasn't allowed to touch or be touched by anyone while she was on her period. Imagine, then, how isolating twelve years of bleeding would have been for her. When Jesus calls her 'daughter' he is publicly reinstating her into the family of God.

We may be tempted to see isolation as old-fashioned and not something that occurs today, but that isn't true. We might not have the same religious and cultural practices, but those with disabilities or chronic illnesses can still find themselves being treated as social outcasts. Not necessarily as a result of malice – possibly simply apathy or unawareness. Sometimes people are incredibly awkward around me in social settings and sometimes they don't want to make the effort to accommodate me. There have been times in my life when social groups have run events that are technically open to me, but are gatherings I'm unable to attend due to accessibility. In society there are still basic things that aren't in place to a sufficient degree for those with disabilities.

The hardest moments for those who are chronically ill are not necessarily when the illness starts. Despite the shock of these life events, sometimes it takes a while to come to terms with them, and to begin with there are often lots of visits and support. The hardest times frequently come months or years after, where you're still contending with your situation, but everyone else has moved on. I've heard similar experiences from those who suffer bereavement. Usually the grief and pain outlive others' sympathy. I don't think that's really a criticism of others, as I'm sure I'm also guilty of having been there for people in the early days, then over time... well, life gets busy. I still care, but I can't give as much time maybe. I think it's probably an unavoidable reality for our extended friendship/acquaintance groups, but it should be a challenge for all of us to not allow that to happen with our closest friends. Thankfully I've had some amazing friends in my life who have been through it all with me.

I think it's essential to say that many disabled people don't want to be healed and I urge Christians and those who pray to be sensitive when offering prayer to people with disabilities. For some, their disability is so intrinsically linked to who they are that they either don't want to be healed or feel they don't need healing. Regardless of what you think about that, if it's how they feel, it is to be respected. They are the ones living with the disability, after all. Not only that, but throughout the Bible Jesus asks the disabled, 'What can I do for you?' He doesn't look at a blind man and assume he wants his sight back. He asks first.

As I've already mentioned, I do believe in healing and I would accept prayer for healing. I believe God's original plan for humanity was to have healthy bodies and fullness of life. For me, it is clear – both theologically and scientifically – that I was designed to walk. If God didn't want me to walk, why create legs? So reverting back to his original plan is always going to be preferable for me. That said, while my life would be easier if I could walk, it wouldn't necessarily be fuller – there are many able-bodied people who are less content than I am. I also realise that there is a good chance physical healing won't happen for me in this life. I may have to wait until the end of time, when he makes all things new.

Do you remember the story I told back in Chapter 2 about being prayed for at a Christian youth festival; when I said that if I was ever healed one day, the first thing I'd like to do was dance? And then I broke down in tears? Well, you'll remember I wasn't healed in that moment. What I didn't tell you was what happened the following year when I returned to the same festival.

I was in one of the evening sessions with my mum, enjoying the worship, and a guy came up to me. I didn't recognise him, but he was looking at me and getting really emotional... it was making me feel quite uncomfortable. He then asked, 'Do you remember me?'

I thought, *Oh, this is so awkward! Do I just admit that I don't?* I looked at him, apologising with my eyes.

He said, 'It's OK! I prayed for you last year for your healing.'

And as he said that, the penny dropped, and I remembered he'd been part of the group that prayed for me. Noticing the tears running down his cheeks, I felt bad for him. I instantly assumed he was disappointed, gutted that I was still in a chair one year on, and the prayers hadn't worked – nothing had changed.

I'll always remember what he said to me, as it completely took me by surprise: 'I'm sorry if this makes you feel awkward with me crying. I'm just so overwhelmed!'

I asked why.

'Because you're still here. You've come back this year.'

I thought, *Well, of course I have... I love these weeks!* So I said, 'I'm sorry. I don't really know what you mean.'

He said, 'Sorry, it's just that your faith is amazing! Yeah, we didn't see you get up out of your chair, but that wasn't the miracle. The miracle is your faith.'

At the time, I'd never really thought about it in those terms before. That was probably one of the first occasions when it occurred to me that the goal isn't physical health. If Jesus is who he says he is, then the goal is being close to Jesus. Everything else is secondary and being close to Jesus offers far more than working legs ever could.

11

Q: If you could go back in time and change what happened to you, would you do it?

A. No, I think I'd still marry him.

Jade

As I've reflected on my life, this question has regularly come to mind. I think it's quite common for anyone who experiences something that is both traumatic and apparently random to ask: 'What if?' What if I hadn't gone to the park that day? What if I'd had a greater level of recovery like most people I know with acute transverse myelitis? What if I was born 300 years later when a cure for paralysis had been engineered?

However, what we often don't do, when we play these mental games, is recognise that it could also work the opposite way. What if I'd become paralysed a few years later, once I'd passed my driving test, and was unable to hit the brake in my car and died in a car crash? What if my paralysis had travelled higher and I'd become tetraplegic? What if I'd been born 300 years earlier, before medical science was capable of performing the multiple operations I've needed that have saved my life so far?

It cuts both ways. Not only that, but I also don't think I would have become the person I am today, had the experiences I've had, or even had the family I have, if it weren't for the accident. My paralysis has made me an incredibly patient person, which is a skill I've needed in absolute spades as a mum to two kids… and a wife to John.

My need for help and my dependency on others has also brought some of the most caring, loving friends into my life. At university, I met people like Luke and Taurai, whose love and support and acts of service enabled me to have a far more 'normal' uni experience than I would otherwise have been able to alone.

My disability has enabled me to inspire other people with a story similar to mine. Most weeks John reads me a message from someone thanking us for modelling interabled relationships in the way we do. What is most heart-warming about those messages is that we're not intentionally trying to model life as an interabled couple. We're just having fun and being real online. It's incredibly flattering that those silly videos have connected with people, not in a fake 'sunshine, rainbows and cotton candy Disney' fashion, but in an honest 'life can be hard, but we can thrive and find joy in the tough times' kind of way.

We began in the opening chapter by talking about fear and worry, and how they hold us back from living the good life, and we made the point that none of us can change our past, but we can worry away our present and limit our future. If I were to become pre-occupied with what could have been, I might miss out on my potential and delay the plans I believe God has in store for me. Instead, I can surrender my circumstances to the one who is never surprised, and choose to face each day knowing that I'm made by God and in God's image, and because of that I have dignity, value and purpose.

This thinking has helped me greatly in my personal life. The power of living from the belief that God has plans for my life that do not require working legs – simply an open heart – is the reason I've managed to keep going, even with the deck stacked against me. Sure, I've been dealt a tough hand, but I've always known that God is bigger than my disability. Sometimes in life we have two choices: it's either give up or get up.

I'd love to say that the resilience I have is a result of sheer strength of character and my own innate brilliance, but first it's not true, and second that's not helpful to anyone else. If it was an innate thing, you would either have it or you wouldn't. I don't believe that's true.

I believe the ability to cope amid suffering, and come out the other side and thrive, is hardwired into all of us. But I also believe we can't do it alone – or at least not for very long. While I'd love to take the credit, I can't. I'm not that strong and I don't mind admitting it.

So how have I managed? Well, I'm not trying to be preachy, but it would be disingenuous for me to take all the credit, because throughout my life I've experienced first-hand that 'in all things God works for the good of those who love him' (Romans 8:28). My faith in God and my belief in his goodness has genuinely never wavered, but I know for some that will be surprising. For many, suffering is the big reason they *don't* believe in God, maybe the reason they left church or have never been. Maybe that's you and you've turned away from God, because you feel he turned away from you. But for me, God wasn't the problem. In fact, he was the only reason I got through my suffering.

Finally, one question that I think is worth us all asking when we wish things hadn't happened the way they did is: 'Had I not gone through this, how would my life be different?' When trauma is raw, this can be an incredibly painful question to ask, but as time goes on, pondering this can actually bring us the hope we need to keep going. Many of the people we admire the most are those who have gone through the greatest adversity. From Martin Luther King Jr to Corrie ten Boom, there seems to be something about resilience that we admire. There is something about pain that helps people go further than they otherwise would have if they'd had an easy life.

Scientists once conducted an experiment to find the perfect growing conditions for trees, fruit and vegetables. They created a biodome with what they believed were the perfect conditions for growth. These included removing all outside threats that nature would otherwise have thrown at them. Everything seemed to be going well until the trees grew to a certain height and just fell over. The scientists were confused by this, until they realised they'd forgotten one crucial factor: wind. Trees need wind, because it strengthens their roots and encourages them to grow deeper. The deeper the roots, the stronger the tree. A tree without wind may grow tall, but only a tree subjected to wind will grow strong. In the same way, we are stronger having suffered. And in my suffering my roots in God grew deeper. I think this was what my parents hoped for me too. When I first became paralysed, they bought me a gold locket, and engraved on the back was, 'Out of little acorns, mighty oak trees grow.'

The way God has blessed my life, always being faithful to his promises, gives me hope for the future. Hope is a great antidote to fear. As Maya Angelou puts it: 'Hope and fear cannot occupy the same space. Invite one to stay.'[1] Hope gets my invitation every time.

1   M. Angelou. X, 8 August 2020: https://twitter.com/DrMayaAngelou/status/129218477987039
6422 (accessed 27 March 2024).

Acknowledgements

We want to start by thanking God – for literally everything. We authored this, but you authored us, the universe and everything in it. We even used your paper. Thank you for giving us the opportunities and making a way for this book to be published. If you could make it a number one best-seller too, that would be amazing. Mostly, thank you for being the one who works all things for good. For taking what could have been a sad story and redeeming it in the way that only you could, bringing beauty from brokenness and purpose from pain.

We want to thank our brilliant editors, Elizabeth Neep and Lauren Windle. Elizabeth for helping us form the project, giving us a clear vision and structure and even the title, and Lauren for picking up the mantle and putting the flesh on the bones, your brilliant notes and additions, for keeping us to deadlines and encouraging us so much that what we were writing wasn't just intelligible, but actually good.

We want to thank our kids for being such fun, strong-willed and loving additions to our family. You've taught us so much about ourselves, you inspire us every day and you're the most entertaining people we've ever made.

Jade

We're going to do some separate acknowledgements now, as you'll be relieved to know we don't share the same parents. I want to thank my incredible dad and mum, Mark and Lydia Greasley, who have tirelessly supported, loved, challenged and motivated me. Now a parent myself, I have a fresh appreciation of how incredibly hard it must have been to see me suffer without being able to prevent it or nurse me back to full health. Dad, thank you for being my theological sparring partner. Without your teaching and debates from an early age, I wouldn't have been anywhere near as well equipped with answers for the big questions or understanding God's plan amid my paralysis. Mum, thank you for teaching me that one of life's most important lessons is to never take yourself too seriously. You taught me that if you can fix it, fix it; if you can't, then laugh. Because of you I was never afraid to give things a go.

I want to thank my sister Amber and brother Michael, for being so understanding and patient. It can't have been easy having a sister who received so much attention – and I don't just mean for my outstanding beauty, hilarious banter and incredible intelligence. Still, at least you can dance better than me, Amber.

I want to thank so many incredible friends who have truly gone the extra mile to love and support me. Gabby Lewis, my Swansea gal, and the Lewis family as a whole. Taurai Bandawa, Luke Aylen, Sarah Pillow, English Elliott, Rachael Newham and Bethanna Hobbs, my uni guys, who not only made life less isolating and more fun, but supported me practically and helped make my uni experience as normal as possible.

I want to thank all the doctors and nurses without whom I might not have been here today. For those in Morriston Hospital and Stoke Mandeville, who not only kept me alive, but also stopped to have a cuppa with me. Thank you for treating me like a person, not just a patient. Thank you also to Luxmi and her tissue viability team in Hillingdon, who not only helped me heal during the most traumatic time of my life, but encouraged me that healing and thriving again was possible.

Thank you to Julian and Sarah Richards, for your love and leadership of Cornerstone Church in Swansea, a church that cared for me so incredibly, prayed for me regularly and supported us a family. Thank you to everyone at Cornerstone who gave me such an amazing experience of church as a child and young adult.

John

I want to thank my parents too, John and Julie Reynolds, who have also been through a lot raising me. You didn't have the same traumatic experience Jade's parents had – I was just incredibly annoying. Thank you for always encouraging my sense of humour and craziness, and for helping me with all the tasks my ADHD makes difficult. Thank you to both sets of parents for all the support you've given us as a family, for sacrificially being there for us even as adults and for helping us with the kids so we could write this book and not go insane.

I want to thank my mentor and friend Simon Cragg for supporting me in my faith, challenging me when needed, but mostly encouraging me to use my gifts; for showing me church didn't have to be serious all the time, that comedy was welcome and laughter was encouraged.

Huge thanks also to my brother Josh and my sister Katie for helping to form my sense of humour; for all the times we cried laughing and for giving me the confidence that comes with being the best-looking sibling.

Thank you to Paul Desai, Paul Wragg and Sam Amos for all the uni laughs, the deep chats and for being normal Christians.

Thank you to Andy Kind for being a great friend and comedy mentor; for not only giving me comedy opportunities when I was still absolutely rubbish, but also paying me while I was still rubbish. Your comedy retreats, the example you set and the heart you have to see faith and comedy go hand in hand have had a bigger impact than you realise.

Thank you to Jason and Rachael Gardner, our current church leaders, for championing us so passionately, encouraging us to step out of our comfort zones and for helping to provide opportunities to use our gifts to make a difference for the kingdom of God. Thank you to everyone at St Luke's Blackburn for helping us settle in the north and for being such a great church family.